RAISING UP
YOUNG
HEROES

DEVELOPING A REVOLUTIONARY

YOUTH MINISTRY

# EFREM SMITH

IVP

InterVarsity Press
Downers Grove, Illinois

*InterVarsity Press*
*P.O. Box 1400, Downers Grove, IL 60515-1426*
*World Wide Web: www.ivpress.com*
*E-mail: mail@ivpress.com*

*InterVarsity Press® is the book-publishing division of InterVarsity Christian Fellowship/USA®, a student movement active on campus at hundreds of universities, colleges and schools of nursing in the United States of America, and a member movement of the International Fellowship of Evangelical Students. For information about local and regional activities, write Public Relations Dept., InterVarsity Christian Fellowship/USA, 6400 Schroeder Rd., P.O. Box 7895, Madison, WI 53707-7895, or visit the IVCF website at <www.ivcf.org>.*

*All Scripture quotations, unless otherwise indicated, are taken from the* Holy Bible, New International Version®. NIV®. *Copyright ©1973, 1978, 1984 by International Bible Society. Used by permission of Zondervan Publishing House. All rights reserved.*

*Design: Cindy Kiple*

*Images: Getty Images*

*ISBN 0-8308-3209-2*

*Printed in the United States of America* ∞

**Library of Congress Cataloging-in-Publication Data**

*Smith, Efrem (Efrem D.), 1969-*
    *Raising up young heroes: developing a revolutionary youth ministry*
    */Efrem Smith.*
       *p. cm.*
    *ISBN 0-8308-3209-2 (alk. paper)*
    *1. Church work with youth. I. Title.*
*BV4447.S59 2004*
*259'.2—dc22*

2004000440

| P | 18 | 17 | 16 | 15 | 14 | 13 | 12 | 11 | 10 | 9 | 8 | 7 | 6 | 5 | 4 | 3 | 2 | 1 |
|---|----|----|----|----|----|----|----|----|----|---|---|---|---|---|---|---|---|---|
| Y | 19 | 18 | 17 | 16 | 15 | 14 | 13 | 12 | 11 | 10 | 09 | 08 | 07 | 06 | 05 | 04 | | |

To my wife, Donecia,

and my two daughters, Jaeda and Mireya.

# CONTENTS

# INTRODUCTION

A few summers ago I took a group of about thirty young people to a leadership conference in Colorado. I partnered with a guy named David Belton, who at the time was working with the Boys & Girls Club in Minneapolis. One of the young people David brought to the conference was Cory, and I won't ever forget him, because for most of the trip he was a major problem. I must have threatened to send him home at least four times that week. I don't even know why David brought Cory on that trip, because he wasn't a Christian and didn't seem at all interested in being a positive leader. Although I kept trying to connect with Cory, I must admit that by the third day of the conference I was pretty much sick of him. His behavior was so negative that I regretted that David had brought him.

Then, on the last night of the conference something unbelievable happened. That night the speaker gave an altar call, which was not expected since this was a Christian conference. Even so, a number of young people began to move forward in response, and I couldn't believe my eyes when I saw Cory up front, crying his eyes out! He became a Christian that night, and I remember staying up late talking with him. He apologized for his behavior and committed to live a new life. On the bus ride back to Minnesota, he was totally different from the guy who had ridden to Colorado with us.

When we arrived back in Minnesota, I gave Cory my number and invited him to get involved with our youth group. Unfortunately, I didn't see Cory again for the next two months. That fall I decided to go to a high school football game not far from the church where I was serving, and as I parked my car next to the field, I noticed a group of boys standing by a tree. When I got out of the car, the boys, who had been doing drugs behind the tree, all ran off except one—Cory. He just looked at me, shocked and embarrassed. I couldn't believe that he was back to living his old life.

Finally, he managed to say, "I tried, man, I really tried." With that he started to walk away. I followed him for a little while and shared some words with him, but we soon parted ways, and I haven't seen him since. I realized then that Sunday school, confirmation, midweek club and youth choir alone weren't enough to reach all the Corys of the world.

Regardless of ethnicity, economic status, family structure or geographic location, youth today are living in a fast-paced, technological, diverse, hip-hop, roller-coaster-of-emotions type of world, and often as youth ministers, we feel like we're just hanging on for the ride. It used to be that school shootings were just an inner-city thing, but then Columbine happened. It used to be that we were safe if we simply stayed away from certain "bad" neighborhoods, but then September 11 happened. In the midst of all this change, young people's minds and emotions and the issues that they face have evolved as well. As a result of technology, postmodernism and multiculturalism, youth ministry has been forced to change. We now have to deal not only with drugs, alcohol and teen pregnancy but also with cutters, graphically sexual and bloody video games and the effects of the increase in divorce rates.

So do we just pray that our youth ministries are never affected by all of these issues, or do we become proactive and develop youth ministries that can raise up young heroes for God in spite of all of the challenges they face? I hope you choose the latter, because that is what this book is about. It's about the use of a holistic approach to youth ministry that fights for the spiritual lives of our young people. (I use the word *fight* because, with all of the people, institutions and systems competing for the attention of young people today, it may take a position of spiritual warfare to reclaim them for Jesus.) My goal for this book is not just to present ideas for a holistic approach to youth ministry but to also present a practical youth ministry model that reaches youth's spirits, souls and bodies.

How can we continue to be effective in youth ministry with the challenges that young people face today? How can we share the Bible with passion, listen to the cries of our young people's souls, teach compassion and justice, focus on intimacy with God as an essential of the Christian journey and get youth to think seriously about their futures—all in one youth group setting?

I believe that today, more than ever, youth ministry must go beyond just Sunday school, confirmation and small groups. None of these things are bad, nor should they be thrown out. But, I believe that with the challenges they face today, youth need out-of-the-box ministry models to teach them to walk daily with Jesus. It's not that there aren't some young people who are living transformed lives, but many of today's youth need a more holistic model of youth ministry, one that understands that altar calls are only the on-ramps to true transformation. After that, young people need us to walk alongside them, seeing them as God sees them, helping them find their spiritual gifts and calls.

The stories, principles and ministry models I share in this book are to that end. In the chapters of this book I will use biblical stories of young heroes along with stories of young people I know who have made and are making a tremendous impact in their circles of influence. In addition, I will present a practical theology and ideas for going beyond just a youth-group model of youth ministry to a revolutionary youth ministry that raises up young heroes for God.

Even today, I still wish I had kept walking with Cory.

# 1

# BIBLICAL
## GOD LOVES YOUNG PEOPLE

God yearns to interact with young people, and he is in the business of using them to do incredible things in the world. The Bible is full of stories that show us just how true this statement is.

*Joshua.* Take, for example, the story of Joshua. As a youth he was sent by Moses to spy out the Promised Land, which was at the time inhabited by what the adults called giants (see Numbers 13). Joshua, along with another young man, Caleb, believed that the people of God could indeed take the land that was promised to them. When the adults felt like grasshoppers, it was the younger generation, Joshua and Caleb, who believed the promises of God. Then, at the end of Moses' life, Joshua was given the call to be strong and courageous as the baton of leadership was handed to him (Deuteronomy 31:7-8). Though he was young he led his people into the Promised Land with shouts, praises, marching and the sound of trumpets (see Joshua 6). God is in the business of using young people as revolutionary leaders.

*David.* Consider the story of young David in the seventeenth chapter of 1 Samuel. There was a giant named Goliath who brought fear and terror upon David's people. The adults who were trained in warfare with swords and shields were afraid to deal with the giant. Yet David, with no sword and no shield—only a slingshot and some stones—took out the giant and brought about victory. God is in the business of using ordinary young people to do extraordinary things.

*Josiah.* What about King Josiah, who is mentioned in 2 Kings 22? He became king when he was eight years old, and even though his father and grandfather before him were evil kings, he broke this curse in his generation by being a king who followed God. He made the Word of God a priority and called his people to revere the Lord's commands once again. "And a little child will lead them" (Isaiah 11:6). God is in the business of using children to do incredible things in the world.

*Esther.* Have you ever really looked at the book of Esther in the Old Testament? This is the story of a girl whom God raises up to become a queen. I'm not talking about some homecoming queen waving to the crowd from a float in the middle of a football stadium. I'm talking about a queen who brought political, social and spiritual change to her land and her people. She risked her life in approaching the king on behalf of her people. And she did this in spite of the fact that she wasn't raised by her biological mother or father. God is in the business of taking a foster girl and developing her into a queen of destiny.

*Jeremiah.* Consider for a moment the book of Jeremiah. In the first chapter God says that he knew the young Jeremiah before he was formed in his mother's womb. Then God tells Jeremiah that there is a calling upon his life to be a prophet to the nations. Jeremiah responds by telling God that he is only a child—as if God didn't already know that! God then tells Jeremiah that the words placed in his mouth will not be his own, but will come from God. He tells Jeremiah that the same God who puts words in his mouth will rescue him in the time of trouble (see Jeremiah 1:5-10). God is in the business of taking kids who are scared, shy and intimidated and giving them the ability to go public with their gifts and speak boldly.

*Timothy.* And then there's a young man in the New Testament named Timothy. His mother was a believer, but his dad wasn't. Yet having one parent who did not believe was not an obstacle for Timothy. His mentor, Paul, saw something in Timothy maybe even beyond what Timothy saw in himself.

> Don't let anyone look down on you because you are young, but set an example for the believers in speech, in life, in love, in faith and in purity. Until I come, devote yourself to the public reading of Scripture, to preaching and to teaching. Do not neglect your gift, which was given you through a prophetic message when the body of elders laid their hands on you. (1 Timothy 4:12-14)

Paul saw Timothy through God's eyes, and Timothy became a leader in church planting and development. God is in the business of using young people as leaders within the church.

When it comes to young people, God goes way beyond just Sunday school, confirmation and weekly clubs full of icebreaker games, pizza and soda. God sees youth—and even little children—through different eyes.

## YOUNG HEROES

On many occasions the disciples had problems with their eye-
sight. Even though they spent a lot of up-close time with Jesus,
there were times when they didn't see the world the same way
he did, especially when it came to youth. Consider the scene
in Matthew 19:13-15:

> Then little children were brought to Jesus for him to
> place his hands on them and pray for them. But the disci-
> ples rebuked those who brought them.
>
> Jesus said, "Let the little children come to me and do
> not hinder them, for the kingdom of heaven belongs to
> such as these." When he had placed his hands on them,
> he went on from there.

The disciples were actually obstacles that were keeping the
little children from getting to Jesus. Are there some churches
that are acting as obstacles in the way of young people getting
to Jesus? Senior pastors who still haven't made youth ministry
a priority? Youth ministers who are on staff but have yet to create strategic plans for their ministries? Could it be that a pre-
dictable approach to youth ministry actually stands in the way
of young people getting into the lap of the Savior?

When you look at young people, what do you see? Just because they're in the church and attend every trip and youth
event doesn't mean they're not dealing with serious issues in
their lives. Are you able to see past the youth-group smiles and
laughter to catch a glimpse of what's really going on in their
lives? Are you able to see past the challenges that seem to have
overtaken them to God's plan and destiny for them?

Going beyond just working with a youth group to actually raising up young heroes for God means that you have to see youth through God's eyes. As youth ministers it is our job to provide opportunities for youth to get up close to Jesus.

## WE'VE LOST SIGHT OF THE POSSIBILITIES

As we've already seen, the Bible is full of stories about God using young people to do incredible, awesome and even dangerous things in order to bring love, justice, peace and transformation to the world. But the examples of young people doing revolutionary things don't end with the stories in the Bible. Even in our contemporary history, youth have been involved in many major political and spiritual movements.

From America to Africa and beyond, young people have been involved in movements to bring positive change to the world. Unfortunately, many churches have stopped calling young people to a Christ-centered, revolutionary movement. In our privileged, technological and postmodern culture, we have lost sight of the potential impact of our young people. We talk to them and nurture them for some future change, some down-the-road impact that they may never even live to see. In the meantime, we have fallen way behind in presenting a gospel that reaches them where they are and calls them to a radical new belief system and a lifestyle that can have an impact on their generation. Instead, we now hear stories of youth taking the lives of others, destroying communities with drugs and committing suicide. Many of them feel neglected, useless and disconnected from the positive impact they could have.

## MINISTRY MODEL

We all know that Martin Luther King Jr. was a key figure in the Civil Rights movement, but what about a little African American girl named Ruby Bridges, who risked her life to be one of the first children to desegregate the public schools in the South? Maybe you already know the story, but please go back down memory lane with me for just a moment. Here was this young girl, putting her life on the line daily just to go to school. She would walk with military escort through a crowd of people who were spitting on her, throwing sticks and rocks at her and yelling at her just for going to school. One day, as she walked through this crowd and made her way up the school steps to the door, she stopped, turned and faced the crowd. It looked like she was saying something to them. When she went into the school one of her teachers asked her what she had said to the crowd, and Ruby replied, "I didn't say anything to them; I was just praying for them." What a young revolutionary for God!

We all know that Nelson Mandela was a key leader in the fight against apartheid in South Africa, but if you've ever seen the movie or the Broadway play *Sarafina*, you've seen that there were also young people in action, risking their lives to bring change to their native land. My wife, Donecia, and I had the opportunity to travel to South Africa and go to a museum that told the history of the fight against apartheid. In that museum were pictures of young people standing for unity and peace with only the weapons of singing, marching and praying. Many of those young people lost their lives in order to bring about a new South Africa.

There are many reasons why our youth are not revolutionary in their Christian thinking and living. One reason is that some church leaders today don't believe that revolutionary movements line up with the Bible. They only see revolutions through the eyes of secular political and social movements and have yet to see the Exodus story or the life and ministry of Jesus as revolutionary movements.

Another problem is that some adult leaders in the church who do believe in movements don't know how to articulate a vision for a new, Christian-based revolution that speaks to the issues that young people face today. In the African American community there are many churches that are struggling to reach their young people even though during the Civil Rights movement, these same churches were full of youth being trained to fight for justice in a Christian-based, nonviolent way.

I want the youth in my church to have memories of a youth group where they may not have had the biggest budget or the largest youth room, but where they witnessed young people just like them getting close to Jesus. And, hopefully, they will get close to Jesus themselves. I don't want them to see the church as just a place where old people connect to God through sermons, prayers and songs and couldn't care less if they connected with anyone under the age of thirty. I want young people to remember more than pizza, crazy games, van rides, messages and prayers. I want them to see the church as a refuge, as a welcoming community that points them to a loving Savior on a level they truly understand, without watering down the authentic message of the gospel. I want them to become adults who have great memories of how the church invested in them as young people. I want them to remember intimate moments with Christ that led them to an authentic realization of who they truly are. I want to be used by God to ignite a revolution in the lives of young people!

## STARTING A REVOLUTION

**Revolt:** to turn from; to take your allegiance from one and give to another.

**Revolution:** a complete change.

**Revolutionize:** to make a drastic change.

Youth are daily bombarded with messages that keep them from being everything God created them to be and pull them away from making a positive impact on the world. Violence, teen pregnancy, sexually transmitted diseases and drug and alcohol abuse are just some of the daily challenges they face, and being active in a youth group doesn't protect them from these struggles. This is exactly why there is a need for a youth revolution.

Before I scare you away with the term *revolution*, I'd better define it. When some people think of revolution, they think of rebellion against what is right. But what about rebelling against the things that seek to destroy the lives of young people? A revolt is about taking your allegiance from one ruler and giving it to another. In this context, revolt means moving our young people's allegiance away from messages, systems and people that destroy them and placing it in God, who loves them and has an awesome plan for their lives that begins right now.

We must take this warfare approach to youth ministry because we are fighting a spiritual battle. "For our struggle is not against flesh and blood, but against the rulers, against the authorities, against the powers of this dark world and against the spiritual forces of evil in the heavenly realms. Therefore put on the full armor of God" (Ephesians 6:12-13). A revolutionary approach that sees ministry as a spiritual battle is the first step in getting beyond a simple youth-group approach and moving toward a holistic approach that provides relevant and practical models of youth ministry.

In this first chapter I have begun with a biblical foundation, and from this foundation I will provide various ways of looking at youth ministry from a broader perspective, using the words *revolutionary, holistic, courageous, warfare, leadership, multiethnic, serving* and *collaboration*. We will go further in depth about these various approaches to youth ministry in following chapters, but it's important to know that the holistic approach serves as the overarching concept, bringing meaning to all the other approaches. Thus, as we talk about the other six approaches, we will do so with the holistic approach as our foundation.

I believe that God has given young people everything they need to build his kingdom and make a revolutionary change in the world. To tap into this potential and influence those around them, youth need only to come into relationship with God through Jesus Christ and embrace his love and purpose for them through the empowerment of a Spirit-filled life.

The truth of Christianity as a revolutionary change of the heart, which should lead to revolutionary change in the world, is the same truth it has always been. But how we call and nurture youth in the revolution may have to change. Youth must be reached out to, nurtured and empowered. Moving beyond a youth-group approach and into a holistic approach that starts a youth revolution may require a change in how you see youth ministry and young people in general, but it's not impossible. Let me help you see how.

# REVOLUTIONARY
## ADULT DREAMS FUEL YOUNG VISIONS

*And afterward, I will pour out my Spirit on all people. Your sons and daughters will prophesy, your old men will dream dreams, your young men will see visions. (Joel 2:28)*

Youth ministry begins with how you see young people. When you look at them, do you see them through the eyes of fear, anger, intimidation, stereotypes or the evening news? Raising up young heroes for God begins with seeing youth as young heroes from the first moment you lays eyes on them. It involves dreaming young-hero dreams for them—even if their current lives aren't very heroic.

In the mid '90s, I was a high school girls' basketball coach at Roosevelt High School in South Minneapolis. I had heard about what a great basketball player Davita was before I even was offered the coaching job—and I had also heard about her behavioral issues. She had been suspended on a number of occasions and was now being sent to an alternative school. But because she lived close to Roosevelt High School, she could still play on the basketball team if the principal would allow it.

That was the major challenge: trying to convince the principal to let Davita play. "No way," he said the first time I asked about the possibility. "She has the worst attitude I've ever seen." He went on to recall every time Davita had gotten herself into trouble over the first few months of that school year and said he was glad to see her go to the alternative school. In response I painted a different picture of Davita, based on what she could be. "Are we talking about the same girl?" the principal asked. I went on to tell him that with the right environment, love and discipline Davita could become a good team basketball player, which would lead to her being a better student. Finally, the principal gave in, with the understanding that if Davita got into trouble in any way, it was my responsibility and she would be immediately kicked off the team.

Things started out rough. Davita's attitude always rose to the surface when things didn't go well in practice, but every time she fell back on her old ways, I reminded her of what I saw in her. I would tell her that I saw a leader, a team player and a young woman who had all the abilities to make not only a tremendous impact on our basketball team, but also off the court in the most important places of life.

Pretty soon I began to see a change in Davita. Because of her leadership on that team we won some games that we probably shouldn't have. I'll never forget the night when our point guard and best player, Nicole, hurt her ankle so badly that she had to leave the game and go to the hospital. Davita looked at the rest of the team and shouted, "Keep your heads up; it's not over! We can win this game if we just believe in ourselves. Now, first let's pray for Nicole." Davita played like never before, and we won that game. The next year Davita did well enough at the alternative school that the principal who had said so many bad things about her the year before let her return to Roosevelt High School.

These positive changes happened not because I'm such a great youth minister but because I saw Davita differently than others saw her. I had spiritual dreams of what the real Davita looked like and helped give her a new vision for her life.

You may be the only person in a youth's life who hasn't given up on him or her simply because you see what others can't or won't. I ask you again, when you look at youth, what do you see? When you look at them do you begin to dream dreams of what they could become, regardless of where they are in life? Your dreams for them could be the fuel they need to have vision for their future.

## THE POWER OF DREAMS

I'm not an expert on dreams, but could it be that our thoughts have an impact on our dreams? If this is true, then how we think about young people affects how we are able to dream for and about them. If we don't even like youth, I would think it would be hard to dream of them becoming young heroes for God.

Young people are smart enough to figure out our real agendas. In our youth ministries, are we really about youth or are we about programs? When youth walk into our churches or ministries, can they sense right away that these are places where young people are loved, where there are adults who have dreams of what they can become? Our ministries should be places of refuge for young people, safe and full of the Spirit of God. Youth should sense that in these places they are important, have a voice and will be loved into becoming great.

Raising up young heroes is about seeing in young people what they can't see in themselves. It's about a faith walk of youth development. I say "faith walk" because of how the author of Hebrews defines faith in the eleventh chapter: "Now faith is being sure of what we hope for and certain of what we do not see" (Hebrews 11:1). Although this verse is talking about faith in God, it also takes faith to see young people the way God does. To raise up young heroes from youth who bring many issues and struggles to the table, we have to be sure of what we hope they can become and certain that God can use them to do great things. It takes faith to see lost, outcast, hurting young people through God's eyes.

No matter what they come from—gangs, unwed pregnancies, tattoo parlors, drug deals—with faith we can see young people doing heroic things in God that make a radical difference not only in their own lives but also in the lives of those around them. I love looking at young people I don't even know and dreaming about what they can become. I look at them and say, "Will that one be the next revolutionary, Christ-centered doctor, lawyer, CEO or teacher?"

## THE POWER OF WORDS

From dreaming we must move next to speaking those dreams to youth on a regular basis. They must hear from out of our mouths what God thinks of them and how he desires to use them in powerful ways right now. Do not assume that the young people in your youth group hear the words, "I love you," "You're special" or "You can do it" on a daily basis. Your youth ministry may be the only place where they regularly hear words of affirmation, encouragement and love. Words are powerful. They make an impact on our lives.

**Negative words.** When I was young, there was a saying that went like this: "Sticks and stones may break my bones, but words can never hurt me." Young people said this as a defense against mean words that were spoken to them on the playground. What's wrong with the saying is that it downplays the power of words. Words indeed don't break our bones, but they can break hearts. They can scar our emotions and quench our spirits.

Many of today's young people are carrying with them the impact and effects of negative words. "You're just like your no-good daddy. He's nothing, and you're going to be nothing." "You're always messing up! You do the same thing over and over again. Can't you do anything right?" "You're not college material." "You're not good enough." "How do you expect to get anywhere with a body like that?"

These words do hurt and can have a lasting, destructive effect. Be careful that negative words don't have free reign in your youth ministry. Deal head-on with teasing that goes too far and putdowns that become personal. Teach young people that words are powerful and have lasting effects.

**Good words.** Negative words are not the only kind of words that affect young people. They are impacted by good words as well: "You can make it." "I believe in you." "I love you." However, be aware that these words, if not followed up with the appropriate actions, could have the same effect as negative words.

Picture a boy who has had to deal with the fact that his parents are divorced. His dad, who no longer lives at home, is supposed to pick up his son on Saturday to go to a baseball game. Earlier in the week his dad had told him on the phone, "I'll pick you up this Saturday, and we'll go to the game. I'm sorry we haven't spent much time together lately. I've been busy with work and all, but you know I love you. I'll see you Saturday." Now, picture the boy an hour after Dad was supposed to have picked him up, looking out the window and hoping for the action needed to back up those good words. Good words become negative when there's no action to support them.

Note also that good words need to be backed by appropriate action. Good-sounding words that are followed up by inappropriate actions can be just as devastating as negative words. It's important for our youth ministries to be full of good words and the appropriate actions to back them up if we are to see the positive revolutionary effect that will become a part of our holistic strategy of youth ministry.

**God words.** There are negative words and there are good words, but let's focus for a moment on a third, even more powerful type of word, the "God" word. Since the beginning, God has spoken words that produce revolutionary results.

*God's word speaks light into darkness:* "And God said, 'Let there be light,' and there was light" (Genesis 1:3). There are young people whose lives are dark, and they need a word spoken into their lives that will produce light.

*The word of God brings freedom from oppression:* "And now the cry of the Israelites has reached me, and I have seen the way the way the Egyptians are oppressing them. So now, go. I am sending you to Pharaoh to bring my people the Israelites out of Egypt" (Exodus 3:9-10). There is liberation and justice in God's words, and he speaks not only to a young person's physical condition but also to his or her spiritual condition.

*We can find identity in the word of God:* "The word of the LORD came to me, saying, 'Before I formed you in the womb I knew you, before you were born I set you apart; I appointed you as a prophet to the nations'" (Jeremiah 1:4-5). How amazing to know that God knew you before you were born! There are young people who are searching for identity, and they need to know that God desires to speak purpose into their lives.

*The word of God speaks direction into our lives:* "The word of the LORD came to Jonah son of Amittai: 'Go to the great city of Nineveh and preach against it, because its wickedness has come up before me'" (Jonah 1:1-2). There are young people who, even though they are rough and rebellious on the surface, desire caring and guiding words for their lives.

Now, God could have kept on speaking the powerful word of light, liberation, identity and direction into the lives of people on earth from the heavenly realms. But, as the Bible story unfolds something even more revolutionary takes place. The Word of God leaves the heavenly realms and comes to earth as flesh: "In the beginning was the Word, and the Word was with God, and the Word was God. He was with God in the beginning. Through him all things were made; without him nothing was made that has been made. In him was life, and that life was the light of men" (John 1:1-4).

People were able to talk to and walk with the Word of God. The Word of God healed people, fed them and delivered them from demonic oppression. But then, they arrested the Word of God. They beat him and spit on him. They put a crown of thorns on his head and nails in his hands and feet. The Word of God died, and for a moment there was no word from God.

But thank God, that's not the end of the story. The Word of God rose to life again. This is good news. No, this is revolutionary news! Do the young people in your youth ministry understand the power of this news? The Word of God is not dead. God has a word for young people, and he wants to speak it into their lives and bring them light, liberation, identity and direction.

## THE WORD OF GOD IS ALIVE

A few years ago, at the end of a family reunion in a small town in Arkansas, our whole family attended a small country church together. Before the service started, the senior pastor walked up to the pulpit and said, "I'd like all the guest preachers to come forward."

There were about six of us guest preachers there that day, and the senior pastor took us back to his office and asked, "Which one of you is going to preach for me this morning?" He looked right at me. "Are you going to preach for me?"

"No," I said. "Pastor, I would love to just enjoy the service."

"Well, which one of you is going to preach for me?" he asked as he looked at the others.

Then the smallest and oldest of the preachers said, "I'll preach for you, Pastor."

With that settled, we left the senior pastor's office and went into the sanctuary for the service. When it was time for the sermon, the little, old preacher got behind the pulpit and delivered a sermon I'll never forget. "Turn your Bibles to the book of Acts," he began. Then he said, "Oh, forget it. I'm going to preach to you this morning on the title 'Jesus Is Alive.' That's right, he's alive, he's alive, he's alive! He's not dead, he's not dead, he's not dead. Now, Elvis is dead, but not Jesus; he's alive! Rock Hudson is dead, oh, you can smell his bones from here, but not Jesus; he's alive! My cousin Earl is dead. He owes me ten dollars, and I ain't never getting it back, cause he's dead, but not Jesus; he's alive! Jesus is alive! J-E-S-U-S is alive!" Then he sat down. That was the end of the sermon.

I thought it was the silliest sermon I had ever heard in my life, but as I thought about it later, I realized that it may have been the most powerful I had ever heard. Jesus indeed is alive, but sometimes the church functions as if the Word of God is dead. The Word of God is alive, and it ought to be a live word spoken to young people through a revolutionary approach to youth ministry. God is still in the business of raising up young people to do incredible things, and our youth ministries are the vehicles he wants to use to deliver this word to this generation of young people. We as youth ministers are the word on the street, because Christ, the alive Word of God, dwells within us. We must be willing to be used by God to deliver a word of light, liberation, identity and direction to the youth under our care.

Through hip-hop culture we see today the power of the word within the youth culture. Hip-hop music and now the poetic spoken word has moved from being an influence primarily in the inner city to being an influence in the suburbs, "baggy pants and all"! Rap artists such as Eminem, Nellie, 50 Cent and Snoop Dogg have become a dominating force on CDs, cable and video. There is something powerful about words from the microphone backed up by a rhythmic bass that moves a generation of young people. But the power of this music genre and culture compare in no way to the Word of God. Can you imagine the power of using the vehicle of hip-hop culture to present the Word of God to this generation of young people? I recommend that if you are not already, you should use holy hip-hop as a ministry tool for the Word of God to speak into the lives of young people. A great place to start is to go online to <www.hiphopzone.com>.

## THE WORD ON THE STREET

A word from God through our youth ministries can spark a youth revolution! One time when I was a speaker at a summer youth leadership camp in New York, I preached a sermon called "Young Heroes for God." I shared stories from the Bible about how God uses young people to do revolutionary things and told the adults in the room that the revolution could begin that night just by them beginning to speak into the lives of the young people at the conference. I told them I knew I was stretching them beyond their comfort zones, but that if they trusted God, there was a word that he wanted to speak through them that night.

Right then adults began to go around praying over and speaking into the lives of young people. One girl cried out and ran up to the front of the room and asked me if she could say something into the microphone. Reluctantly, I let her speak to the rest of the group, and she said that one of the adult leaders had just been praying over the girl and told her what a great Bible teacher she could be. The girl explained that she had cried out because she had a desire to teach the Bible but had been afraid to say so because she thought she was too young and would sound silly. Then, one by one, young people began to share on the microphone the power of God speaking into their lives through caring Christian adults. This went on for at least an hour. I've never experienced anything quite like that camp. A revolution began when young people heard something from God specifically for their lives.

A revolutionary youth ministry begins by seeing young people with God's eyes. We must see things in young people that others cannot. We must dream dreams about what they can become and the impact that they can make right now. We must believe in them even when they don't believe in themselves. Then, we must be willing to be used by God to speak light, liberation, identity and direction into their lives based on the Word of God. Take time out of your week to go beyond planning programs for youth group and pray for a revolution to take place in your ministry. Ask God for his eyes. Ask God for the right dreams, and then ask him for the right words.

## ❸

# HOLISTIC
### REACHING SPIRIT, SOUL AND BODY

Youth ministry ought to be formed of strategic plans that have measurable outcomes. The key to a strong ministry is not the programs we implement, but rather the plans that provide foundations for those programs. Now, you might think I'm sounding too corporate, moving to some sort of business model and away from a practical theology for youth ministry. But consider the story of the feeding of the 5,000 as it is found in John 6: "When Jesus looked up and saw a great crowd coming toward him, he said to Philip, 'Where shall we buy bread for these people to eat?' He asked this only to test him, for he already had in mind what he was going to do" (John 6:5-6). Jesus, though he asked his disciples how they might address the crowd's physical hunger, already had a strategy in mind to accomplish just that. He was clear on his desired outcomes and the strategies that would produce them. In the same way, we ought to have strategies in mind for youth ministry.

## WHOLE IN THE IMAGE OF GOD

A youth ministry with positive measurable outcomes has at its foundation a connection between Paul's concern for the whole person in 1 Thessalonians 5:23 ("May God himself, the God of peace, sanctify you through and through. May your whole spirit, soul and body be kept blameless at the coming of our Lord Jesus Christ") and the creation of humanity as it is depicted in Genesis 1:27 ("So God created man in his own image, in the image of God he created him"). God is three in one—Father, Son and Spirit—and since we are made in his image, we can see ourselves as three in one as well: spirit, soul and body.

I don't use this three-part concept to compartmentalize people. I realize that a whole person is a much more complex combination of heart, soul, mind, body and spirit than what I am presenting here. But I use this holistic approach in order to make the ministry models I suggest easier to understand. Let's then take a closer look at these three parts:

*Spirit.* This is the innermost part of a human being, the place where true intimacy with God occurs. This is where the essence of praise and worship takes place. This is where a deeper knowing beyond what the mind is capable of happens. The spirit is the holy of holies in a human being.

*Soul.* The soul is an inner place in a human being, deeper than the body but not as deep as the spirit. It is made up of three parts in itself—the mind, the emotions and the will—and we should not underestimate the power and connection of these three parts. Many choices are made at the intersection of Think Avenue and Feel Street.

*Body.* The body is the outer person. It includes our senses of smell, touch, taste and sight, as well as our physical hungers, thirsts and desires. But the body is not just the flesh that we need to die to daily (see Ephesians 2:3); it's also the part of us that needs health care, shelter, food and water.

As fallen humanity, our spirits are dead until we come into relationship with God through Jesus Christ. We are only two-thirds whole without the regeneration of our spirits, and this causes dysfunction in our souls and bodies. The experience of becoming a Christian begins with our spirits and leads us on a journey toward wholeness in all areas of our lives.

## BEYOND THE SPIRIT

A holistic youth ministry considers the entire person, yet in churches today we can be "so heavenly minded that we're no earthly good," as I once heard an older preacher say. We can focus so much on our young people's spiritual lives that we overlook issues like struggles with body image, thoughts of suicide, sadness over the divorce of parents or lack of health care. Sadly, we often react to the more holistic issues only after a tragedy has already taken place. We know what to do after a school shooting, but we must begin learning how to prevent shootings in the first place by having ministry models in place to reach out to the angry or depressed outcasts who contemplate such violent acts.

We may help a young person to invite Jesus into her heart, but can we afford to not address the fact that she lives without health care, adequate shelter or hope? We may help our youth grow in their knowledge of Jesus, but can't we also minister to them by working with them to pass the basic standard skills test? This is not to say that people's lives have to be paradise on earth in order to make the claim that they are saved and that

## MINISTRY MODEL

We see in the Bible that the ministry methods Jesus used took into consideration the *whole* person:

> Jesus went through all the towns and villages, teaching in their synagogues, preaching the good news of the kingdom and healing every disease and sickness. When he saw the crowds, he had compassion on them, because they were harassed and helpless, like sheep without a shepherd. Then he said to his disciples, "The harvest is plentiful but the workers are few. Ask the Lord of the harvest, therefore, to send out workers into his harvest field." (Matthew 9:35-37)

He taught in the synagogues, which means he engaged people's minds. He preached about the kingdom, which touched the minds and reached the spirits of those who heard him. He demonstrated his concern for the physical welfare of people by the many healings he performed.

Jesus is actively working in their life through the Holy Spirit. The issue here is more for us as the ones ministering to young people. We should wrestle with questions such as these: When a student in our ministry becomes a Christian do we treat it as an ending point or as a beginning point? If we treat it as an ending point we miss the opportunity to walk with them on a more holistic, lifelong journey. Similarly, if a young person doesn't experience God's love and grace beyond a spiritual experience at the altar, are we truly doing youth ministry? If a young person asks forgiveness from God for their past and present sins but doesn't speak to God about their future in all areas of their life then we've failed at helping them understand that our relationship with God is not event-oriented as much as it is a long-term love affair intended to reach every area of our being. We must be proactive in developing youth ministries that impact young people in ways that affect every area of their lives. We must follow Jesus' model and engage our youth on all levels—spirit, soul and body.

## FROM PROGRAMMATIC TO DEVELOPMENTAL

By looking at the areas of spirit, soul and body and taking into consideration things such as setting (urban, suburban, rural) and issues that youth in your ministry are facing, you will have reasoning behind the types of programs and services your youth ministry provides. Within this holistic approach to youth ministry, strategic initiatives can be developed, which give direction to ministry models and lead to measurable outcomes. This moves a youth ministry from a youth-group model with a programmatic foundation to a developmental model, which focuses on the holistic development of young people.

At Park Avenue Methodist Church in Minneapolis, where I served as a pastor of youth and community outreach, I was able to be a part of a church that has had a commitment to holistic youth ministry since the 1960s when they hired a youth pastor named Art Erickson. His job was to spend 50 percent of his time with the youth in the church and the other 50 percent with unchurched youth in the surrounding community. Today Park Avenue has built on this history in some significant ways, and it's not because they're the largest Methodist church in the state of Minnesota or because they have the biggest budget.

Let me share some of the ways that they provided holistic ministry to young people while I was on staff; these are things that still go on there today.

*Spirit: the importance of intimacy.* While at Park Avenue I felt that the best thing I could do for the young people was to find practical ways to help them understand the importance of intimacy with God, the nurturing of their spirits. With this in mind, I planned a spiritual retreat at a campsite about an hour away from the city. On the first night we played games, ate candy and drank soda. If we had taken a vote that night, I would have been named the greatest youth pastor in the world.

The next day, however, was different. After breakfast, I gave each of them a Bible, some paper and a pen and said, "Today we're not going to play a bunch of games like yesterday. I want you to spend some time alone with God."

Many of them looked at me like I was crazy. "What am I supposed to do?" one student asked.

"I don't know," I responded. "That's between you and God." So the kids went out to be alone with God, and I must admit that I was nervous. I had never tried anything like that before.

A couple of hours later when the kids came back, I asked if anyone wanted to share about his or her experience. One girl said that she had read Psalms and that it sounded like poetry. Then she read some poetry that she had written in response, and it was beautiful. A boy said that he had written a rap song, and the next thing we knew, he was performing it for us. One by one other young people began to share about the time they had spent alone with God, and I began to realize that God could do things with young people that I couldn't. It had taken me over ten years in youth ministry to realize that. I had read books and gone to workshops about game ideas and service projects, but up until that point I had never thought about simply teaching kids how to be alone with God.

Sometimes we get so busy with building up a youth group that we forget that teaching youth the discipline of spiritual intimacy is the key to raising up young heroes for God. Our relationships with God are ultimately beyond our intellects and emotions. The spirit of a person is where true praise, worship, meditation and prayer happen. It is through intimacy with God that true faith is built. Within our youth ministries we must focus on the development of the spirit and challenge our young people to seek intimacy with God.

*Equipping and nurturing the soul.* Earlier I laid out three different areas that make up the soul: the mind, the emotions and the will. In order to have a holistic youth ministry, we must take each of these into consideration.

*Mind.* Park Avenue has a strong model of faith-based academic support and enrichment. For one, it has a homework room where students can study and get help with their homework (a great way for adults to volunteer if they have a limited amount of time to donate). We shouldn't assume that youth use their school libraries or that their homes are great study environments, and it doesn't take a big budget to create a space in a church building for this purpose.

They also have a Computer Learning Center, where youth can use computers for homework, balancing their personal budgets and even doing website design. The center allows young people, who are growing up in an increasingly technological world, to learn to use technology in a healthy and positive way. A computer center may sound expensive, but that is not necessarily the case; churches can write grant letters for funding or ask local businesses to donate computers or funds.

It is important for us to care about the academic development of the youth in our ministries. How much better positioned will they be to fulfill God's will for their life if they have succeeded in the area of education?

*Emotions.* Young people are like teakettles when it comes to their emotions. They need a place to let off steam when life gets hot. While working at Park Avenue, I had the opportunity to partner with a ministry called Tree House, which reaches out to at-risk teens in first- and second-ring suburbs of the Twin Cities in Minnesota. Since the youth group I was working with was very diverse and came from all over the Twin Cities area, I thought it would be helpful to observe Tree House's ministry model. What I found was an approach to ministry that really deals with the emotions of young people. Tree House understands that listening to kids earns leaders the right to later speak into the lives of those kids in powerful ways. They use weekly support groups as a way to help young people express their feelings and unpack their emotional baggage.

At one meeting, I sat in a room with an adult leader and about ten young people and observed a model that I believe should be implemented in local church youth ministries as well. The adult leader went around the room and asked the youth to give their names, two words to describe how their weeks were going and to rate on a scale of one to ten how their days were going. Then he asked them if they needed time to talk that night. Before they started talking, the leader asked the young people to set the rules for the night. They came up with rules such as "one person talks at a time," "respect others' views," "don't use real names when telling stories" and "don't take what is said here outside of the room unless there are legal ramifications." As the young people shared their stories, I saw them being liberated as they released the pain, struggles and frustrations from their lives. No one offered answers to their problems, but there is something about the power of being heard that builds community between youth and adults. Because that leader was a good listener, he earned the right to later present the gospel to those youth in powerful ways.

Unfortunately, many adults in youth work are very good at talking but not very good at listening. Maybe you are wondering why it is that after you've spent so much time in prayer about what you will say to your youth group on Sunday, feeling that it is truly a word from God, the young people aren't connecting with you. Have you considered that they may not be connecting because they're distracted by their parents' divorce, breakups with boyfriends or girlfriends, body images, the death of a friend or any other assortment of issues? You may need to develop support groups that are specific to issues that youth are dealing with. You may need to seek out partnerships and networks with counseling or recovery ministries that provide services that your ministry may not have the capacity to deal with. Whatever the case, youth ministries must be positioned to deal with the emotional issues that become barriers to young people's ability to connect to God.

*Will.* Intentionally ministering to young people academically and emotionally leads to the development of the third area of the soul, the will, or the way they make decisions. When youth understand that God seeks to have a relevant place in every area of their lives, that he has a plan for them (see Jeremiah 29:11), it can have a positive effect on the choices that they make.

A few years before coming to Park Avenue I began my youth ministry career at Hospitality House, a Christian boys and girls club. In this first full-time youth ministry job I met a young man named Calvin, who was in the ninth grade. Calvin loved coming down to the center where I served and was involved on our Southside basketball team, our Tuesday Night Talk (T.N.T.) club and our Career Exploration program. I did a lot of listening to the issues that Calvin and the other boys in T.N.T. were going through, and in Career Explorations we helped him and the others think through what they were going to do after high school. These ministries were designed to strategically develop the souls of young people, and by tying in the spiritual with these areas, we were able to help Calvin and others see how God cared about every area of their lives. I believe this led to the positive choices Calvin has made in his life. Today he is close to completing a degree at a Christian college.

As youth workers we need to have a presence in the intellectual and emotional areas of young people's souls so they can see that God desires them to make choices (use their wills) based on his presence in every area of their lives.

**Body talk.** A holistic approach to youth ministry must take into consideration the issues that affect young people's bodies and help youth understand God's plan for their bodies. What does it really mean to see one's body as the temple of God (see 1 Corinthians 6:19)?

### How do we address issues like the lack of health-care coverage in a young person's home?

At Park Avenue Methodist Church they're addressing problems like this through a partnership with the Saint Mary's Health Clinic, a Catholic social service organization with a free clinic that is offered once a week for two hours in the afternoon. Doctors and nurses volunteer to provide free health-care services to children, youth and their families in the surrounding neighborhood. Last year alone they served over two hundred families without health-care coverage. Just think what a group like this could do if they were open all week!

### How do we help young people to have fun, active social lives in ways that glorify God?

One way to reach the area of body is through dance. Unfortunately, today it is hard for young people to find examples of dancing that are not sexual in nature. Couple that with the fact that some churches simply outlaw dancing of any kind, and young people in the church get the sense that anything they do with their bodies is bad. When I served as a youth pastor at Ginghamsburg United Methodist Church in Tipp City, Ohio, we hosted a social alternative for youth called Ultra Live. It was a teen coffeehouse and nightclub that featured DJs playing Christian hip-hop, house and other forms of dance music, as well as food, table games and videos. It took some time for the youth to start dancing, but once they did it was a great way for them to use their bodies in a party setting to give praise to God. Through Christian dance parties and coffeehouses, we are able, in a fun way, to help young people have active social lives and still use their bodies to glorify God.

### How do we address the pressures youth face concerning sexuality and body image?

We must take more time to talk with our young people about body images from a biblical perspective. We can't be afraid to deal with the issue of sexuality in the Bible. We can't shy away from the fact that young people are bombarded with sexual images through music, movies and videos on a regular basis. We must help them deal with these pressures from a Christian perspective.

I especially want to say something in this area about girls. I'm concerned about the images of female bodies being used to sell beer, cars and other products that bombard them on a regular basis. I am concerned about the pressure they feel to look like the women in the magazines or the movies. We need women who will come alongside girls and raise them up as modern-day Queen Esthers.

We must also be willing to deal with other things that affect the body, like sports. I've had wrestlers in my youth group who have done crazy things to make a certain weight class. I'm concerned about the things youth put their bodies through just so that they can make the varsity sports team.

I believe a sports-focused ministry can address many of these body issues and play a major role in a holistic approach to youth ministry. Working as the urban ministry director for the Minnesota Fellowship of Christian Athletes while also serving as a basketball coach at Minneapolis Roosevelt High School gave me a platform for helping young people deal with body issues and allowed me to minister to youth specifically through sports. Sports as ministry lets us focus on more than just winning and losing and can raise more important issues such as physical health, character, and the building of community and unity through a team approach to life. For girls, sports ministry can be a way to help them have a body image that isn't dominated by sensuality. Many statistics show that girls who are involved in sports are less likely to be sexually active and get pregnant.

These questions and examples of ministry don't cover all body issues, but they are a start in looking at how to include the body in a holistic approach to youth ministry.

## TOWARD BIBLICAL YOUTH DEVELOPMENT

In this chapter I have laid out the various examples of a holistic approach to youth ministry not so that you will try to do all of the things mentioned above, but so that you will think through what part your ministry can play in the goal of reaching the whole person when it comes to young people. We must seek to go beyond the youth group to reach young people's spirits, souls and bodies. The gospel ought to have an impact in every area of a young person's life, and we are responsible for helping to make that happen.

A holistic approach can also help in setting long-term ministry goals and bringing about results that will stay with youth through adulthood. We should design our youth ministry based on a picture of what we would want to accomplish with young

people if they were with us from the beginning of middle
school through their graduation from high school. I know this
picture won't fit for every young person, since youth come into
our ministries at different stages of life. But what this long-term
strategic design and picture will do is give us a developmental
sense of youth ministry. I think sometimes we hide behind the
word *ministry* and use it as an excuse for not ministering to the
whole person. But our goal should be youth *development* based
on biblical principles, not just youth ministry.

Ultimately we are called to raise up disciples. Discipleship
is about spiritual growth and maturity. How do we minister to
young people in a way that helps them grow in every area of
their being? Is this what ministry is truly about? Is this what
Jesus was truly about? There has been much debate within the
church over the years about a social gospel approach to ministry versus an approach based more on personal salvation. Both
sides use Scripture—especially the actions and words of
Jesus—to make their point. And to a certain extent both are
right. Jesus is about salvation, and we should not belittle this
point in any way. But he's also about the poor, the sick and the
outcast and how their lives can be changed right now. Jesus'
method of ministry on earth included the whole person—and
so should our methods with young people. A holistic approach
to youth ministry allows us a better opportunity to develop disciples and raise up young heroes for God.

# 4

# COURAGEOUS
## RAISING BOYS TO TAKE ON GIANTS

$G$od uses youth throughout the Bible to bring about social, political and, most importantly, spiritual change in the world. Young people are gifted, and through God they can be actively involved in the harvest field (see Matthew 9:35-38). They can assist adult Christians in taking on the giant issues of today, such as poverty and racism, as well as participate in roles of teaching, worship and other leadership roles that are normally considered for adults only. But we must prepare them for these roles by helping them cultivate a courageous spirit that flows out of intimacy with God.

## LIONS ARE NOT HOUSEHOLD PETS

Lions are dangerous. They have sharp teeth and claws and cannot be treated like the cute little cats we keep as house pets. Occasionally on talk shows animal experts are brought on as guests, and they bring exotic animals with them. When we watch a lion under the care of a trainer we begin to feel more comfortable about it. Maybe it isn't as dangerous as we thought. But then something startles the lion, and it snarls and growls, showing us its true nature. The same is true of spiritual lions in the lives of our young men. Boys may think their lions are cute, to be kept around as pets, or they may think they have their lions trained. Then, when the pressures of life take over, the lions show their true colors.

When young David encountered the lion (I will tell this story in more detail in the following paragraphs), he was taking care of his father's business, and he didn't treat the lion like a house pet. He realized that it was dangerous to him and to the calling he had been given by his father, so he killed it. God has a call on the lives of our young men. That call may be as simple as graduating from high school, but the lion of under-achievement will try to creep in and thwart that call. Like David, our boys must understand that there is an enemy who seeks to keep them from fulfilling their intended calling. They must become lion-killers through intimacy with God and the strength that it provides. Lions aren't meant to be kept around as pets. We must teach boys not to let lions roam in their spirits.

## LION STORIES

It is interesting to see that the Bible describes the devil as a lion: "Be self-controlled and alert. Your enemy the devil prowls around like a roaring lion looking for someone to devour. Resist him, standing firm in the faith" (1 Peter 5:8-9). Our souls are places where the lion will attempt to roam, and we must be prepared to deal with it. But, not only does this Scripture talk about the lion; it also points to our deliverance, which comes through faith, and our faith is strengthened through intimacy with God.

There are many stories in the Bible about young men's encounters with lions, and the principles that they teach apply to the needs of our young men today. Through their intimacy with God, David, Benaiah and Joshua all experienced deliverance from the paw of the lion, and those experiences equipped and empowered them to fulfill God's call on their lives.

*From lions to giants.* In 1 Samuel 17:32-37 we read the following story:

> David said to Saul, "Let no one lose heart on account of this Philistine; your servant will go and fight him."
>
> Saul replied, "You are not able to go out against this Philistine and fight him; you are only a boy, and he has been a fighting man from his youth."
>
> But David said to Saul, "Your servant has been keeping his father's sheep. When a lion or bear came and carried off a sheep from the flock, I went after it, struck it and rescued the sheep from its mouth. When it turned on me, I seized it by its hair, struck it and killed it. Your servant has killed both the lion and the bear; this uncircumcised Philistine will be like one of them, because he has defied the armies of the living God. The LORD who delivered me from the paw of the lion and the paw of the bear will deliver me from the hand of this Philistine."
>
> Saul said to David, "Go, and the LORD be with you."

Young David felt confident about his battle with the giant Goliath because he had experienced the deliverance of God when he met the lion and the bear. He was able to trust that he could count on that same deliverance in his encounter with Goliath. In the same way, a young person who has dealt with the lions and bears in his life will be able to confidently face the giants that come along. Today's boys need to find the same intimacy with God and the resulting courage as they face both private and public battles on a daily basis.

*Hidden pits.* In the book of 1 Chronicles, after David became king, one of his mighty men, Benaiah, went down into a pit on a snowy day and killed a lion (see 1 Chronicles 11:22). By himself, in a pit, he experienced private deliverance and victory. Daniel was thrown into a den of hungry lions for an entire night, and yet in the morning he was still alive. In spite of very bad odds, Daniel experienced in the den, all by himself, the God of deliverance (see Daniel 6:16-23).

There are many young men today who are living in private dens of fear, sadness, depression or anger, and they often have a hard time talking about what's really going on in their lives. They are impacted by the media, so immersed in video games and other types of visual, no-talk stimulation that verbal communication can be a challenge for them, and they struggle to talk about internalized pain because of the tough exteriors they've been conditioned to wear. They face issues all alone in the pits of life and desperately need to know that God is their deliverer. They need to know that God sees their pain, their struggles and their need for personal victory in the areas of their lives that are private from others. When they experience the comfort and intimacy of God in their private lives, they will find a greater ability to take on their public calls.

*Public credibility.* These biblical lion stories remind me of an experience that Steve Floyd, a friend of mine, had during a trip to Africa. In a village in the central part of Africa, he had the opportunity to experience a traditional rite-of-passage cere-mony. As part of the requirements to attain manhood in the eyes of the adults, the boys of the village are sent out in groups of five to kill a lion. Four of the boys in each group get a weapon and one does not. They must find a lion that is asleep, and the boy without a weapon must wake up the lion and get it to chase him. Then the other boys jump out with their weap-ons and kill it. The boy without a weapon is given the lion's mane, because he showed the most bravery, and each of the other four boys gets to keep one of the lion's paws. When the boys return to the village the chief declares them all men.

The point of this story is not that boys need to kill something in order to become adults, but it does illustrate the principle that as Christians we must deal with the lions in our personal lives in order to be able to serve and advance the kingdom of God in our public lives. Our personal relationship with God will have an impact on our credibility in the eyes of the world, which has an affect on our public ministry.

## JOEY THE GIANT-SLAYER

As a boy I had dreams of preaching to people. I had a sense of God's call on my life even at that early age. But I also had a lion of lust that I was never taught to deal with. It caused me to de-sire sex over intimacy with God and a life of purity, and I gave up my virginity in high school. I knew what I had done was wrong, but I didn't know how to deal with that personal lion. Sex wasn't talked about much in the church I grew up in, so I really didn't know who I could talk to in order to get a Chris-tian perspective. I thought I was too messed up to fulfill God's public call for me to preach, and I began to live two separate lives: my social life with my friends and my church life. My lion kept me from sharing my church life and my belief in God with my friends, because the way I was living would have contradicted what I was sharing verbally. My inability to deal with my personal lion affected my ability to believe I could have a public ministry.

Then in my sophomore year of high school I met a boy named Joey. Not only did he go to church like I did, but there was something about his life that I was drawn to. Throughout the school year I watched him share about Jesus with others. I couldn't believe how boldly he shared his faith and the impact that it had. Many of my own friends began to live differently as they spent time around Joey. During our senior year of high school the impact of Joey's public ministry became even more evident. That year a classmate of ours named Pedro was beaten to death after school, and the tragedy rocked our school to the core. Even the teachers were inconsolable, but Joey got up on the stage and spoke to the whole student body. He said that the best way that we could pay tribute to Pedro's life would be to change the way we lived. He boldly stood on that stage and presented the gospel to the entire school. Nobody complained about the separation of church and state that day. You could have heard a pin drop in that auditorium.

As I hung out even more with Joey we began to have a lot of deep conversations. I told him about my calling and about my struggles. I asked him if he had any struggles of his own. He said he had many, and I asked him how he dealt with them. At first his answers were typical: prayer and Bible study. I was doing those things myself, but they didn't seem to be helping much. Then he told me one I hadn't heard before: accountability. He told how he met with his youth pastor, Bart Campolo, on a weekly basis to talk about the issues going on in his life, and how important it was to having a caring adult in his life whom he could trust. He also talked about friends who served as peer accountability partners. Joey understood that we're not supposed to deal with the lions of life by ourselves. These deep conversations transformed me by not only helping me understand my personal lions, but also helping me understand how to fight and experience deliverance.

There is a connection between the courage of David, Joshua and Joey in terms of how they saw giant issues. When the adult Israelites saw the people inhabiting the Promised Land as giants, Joshua saw them differently. He was focused on God's promise instead of on the giants in front of him. The same is true in David's case. His focus was not on Goliath's size but on his personal relationship with God. And when Joey looked at the giant student body in the auditorium that day, he wasn't intimidated by the situation because of his relationship with God. His private belief impacted his public platform and changed my life and the lives of many others.

## HELPING BOYS FACE THE LION'S DEN OF LIFE

If you are in youth ministry, you must understand that you are in a battle with the ultimate lion (Satan) as you work to raise up boys who are able to deal with their own private lions, which are the devil's schemes to thwart boys' credibility and prevent them from being effective in building God's kingdom.

We must present to boys a theology of God as deliverer at a level that they can understand. We must teach them and equip them with the truth that through Jesus Christ the Father desires to have a private, intimate relationship with them and through that relationship to give them the means of defeating the lions in their lives. They must understand that there is no issue so bad that God cannot deliver them. In the book of Exodus, Moses was overwhelmed with the task of confronting Pharaoh and demanding that the Israelites be set free, but through an intimate relationship with God he found strength and courage to take on the task. In order to help students fight their personal lions, we must work into our youth ministries opportunities for students to encounter the Deliverer in intimate, personal ways.

*Adult mentors.* If young people are going to be able to recognize and deal with their personal lions, it's going to be in part because they have adults in their lives who spend time with them. They need to be in long-term, mentoring relationships with caring, Christian adults who are not their parents. Mentors are not there to replace parents, but most youth don't tell their parents about many of the things they are dealing with. In youth ministry, presence is more powerful than programs.

*Peer accountability.* Peer pressure is a major factor behind the decisions that many young people make. It is also through peer pressure that teens give their lions free reign. Many leaders today are finding that going to church on Sunday is not enough for teens to fight the daily battle of pressures, challenges and temptations. Positive peer accountability can provide support and combat the negative peer pressure that young people face. Hanging out with Joey not only connected me to a caring adult mentor but also connected me to new friends who provided positive peer accountability as I dealt with my personal lions.

**MINISTRY MODEL**

When I began go to youth group with Joey, I connected with Bart Campolo. Soon, every Tuesday Bart would pick up Joey, another boy named Julian and me after school and take us to Burger King. We had Whoppers, Pepsis and Bible studies right there in that Burger King in South Minneapolis. From time to time I met one-on-one with Bart to talk more in depth about my personal lions. We talked about dating, relationships, marriage and sex, and Bart didn't judge me. He just asked me a lot of questions—about choosing a girlfriend, what I wanted to do when I grew up and how I was planning to get there. It was so cool to have an adult in my life besides my parents who I could talk so openly with, and spending time with him helped me develop a strategy to deal with my lions.

Many adult males whom I've talked with say they find that living a life of accountability is easier said than done. They understand the importance of accountability but struggle to put it into action as they try to balance careers, family and alone time with God. They did not have peer accountability at a young age and so they find it hard to build in this accountability time in adulthood. Youth ministry must go beyond just a youth group to a youth community in which students care about one another and hold each other accountable. We must teach them when they are young to seek accountability so they have a better chance of living it out as adults.

*Men's ministry.* Boys need a refuge where they can cry, be angry, be real and take off their masks. This is especially true for boys who don't have fathers in the home. They need to know through the presence of a caring adult that God does not desire them to walk through life dealing with issues alone. If you don't already have a men's ministry in your church, start one, not only so that the men in your church know that it's not too late for them to deal with their lions, but also so that they can become mentors to the boys in your community. I also recommend retreats and getaways for boys only.

## GIANT-KILLERS AND LION-SLAYERS

I believe that boys have the abilities and the gifts to bring down the giants of racism, world hunger, poverty, violence and many other important battles in the work of building God's kingdom. They have what it takes to defeat the giants that terrorize the adults who have been trained for battle but are afraid to fight, and our youth ministries can be places where these courageous boys are raised up through holistic developmental strategies. However, these boys will not be as effective as they could be if they don't deal with the lions in their personal lives. The same God whom empowers them to defeat the giant first wants them to understand that they can find victory and deliverance over the lion as well.

## 5

# WARFARE
### RAISING UP YOUNG QUEENS

In 1998 I served as the head boys' basketball coach at Patrick Henry High School in North Minneapolis. They hadn't had a state tournament appearance since 1945, but that year we went to the state championship game, where we lost by only nine points. (The boys' basketball team at Patrick Henry High School went on to win the state championship three years in a row.) The girls' team that year was a different story. They lost every game they played; their most painful match-up ended in a 26-120 loss! I'll never forget the looks on those girls' faces as they walked off the court in front of a gym full of people who were laughing and making fun of them. Many of the girls were not able to hold back their tears.

At the end of that year I moved to a pastorate in Ohio. Then, two years later I returned to the youth pastorate at Park Avenue Methodist Church and was asked to come back and serve as the head girls' basketball coach at Patrick Henry. I had not been able to forget the image of their painful loss two years earlier, so I accepted the challenge wholeheartedly. I wanted the girls to see themselves as winners. The problem was that they had the opposite kind of images in their minds. I was committed to changing how those girls were perceived, but the first thing I had to do was change how they saw themselves.

## HOW GOD SEES GIRLS

The world says that if a girl's body doesn't look a certain way, then she's not beautiful. It says that if she doesn't act a certain way, she won't be acceptable to others. The images girls are expected to live up to come through television, magazines and music, and they often contradict the image that they are truly made in (see Genesis 1:27) and the plan God has for their lives.

If a young woman's view of herself is to be healthy and holistic, it must be based on an intimate relationship with God. Her identity and purpose should be shaped by her spirit. If the spirit is not in ultimate control, then the soul or the body will instead be the primary source of a girl's sense of identity and purpose. For example, if a girl sees herself through the world's eyes and believes that her identity is determined by her body, she may wear revealing clothing in the hope of getting attention and what she believes to be love. But, if she sees herself through God's eyes, as a young queen, she will know that true love and acceptance come through healthy relationships with God and others. As youth leaders we must proactively show girls the difference between how God sees females and how the world sees them.

There is a story in the Bible that demonstrates this very difference:

Then a man named Jairus, a ruler of the synagogue, came and fell at Jesus' feet, pleading with him to come to his house because his only daughter, a girl of about twelve, was dying. . . .

While Jesus was still speaking, someone came from the house of Jairus, the synagogue ruler, "Your daughter is dead," he said. "Don't bother the teacher any more."

Hearing this, Jesus said to Jairus, "Don't be afraid; just believe, and she will be healed." . . .

Meanwhile, all the people were wailing and mourning for her. "Stop wailing," Jesus said. "She is not dead but asleep."

They laughed at him, knowing that she was dead. But he took her by the hand and said, "My child, get up!" Her spirit returned, and at once she stood up. (Luke 8:41-55)

Though the people around the little girl thought she was dead, Jesus had a different view. Though many people saw the girls' basketball team at Patrick Henry as losers, I had a different perspective.

## DEALING WITH FALSE IMAGES

When I took over coaching the girls' basketball team, I had to deal with the false images that were oppressing the girls with the idea that they were losers. I also had to deal with the fact that the loser image was there in part because their past actions backed up how they were presently being perceived. And I had to deal with the fact that some of the people who felt negatively about the girls were people within their own school. Let's take these three issues one at a time.

*Culture.* So many of the images that girls see or hear are sexual in nature. I was riding in my car one day listening to a popular radio station, and I decided to see how many songs I had to listen to before I heard one that had nothing to do with sex. Most of the songs were sung by females, and by the time I arrived at my destination I still hadn't heard a song that didn't refer to sex in some way. Most teenagers listen to a lot of music. If they're listening to the same songs I heard, what images are going through their heads? I'm not trying to say that all secular music is bad, but we must understand that the music and movies our culture produces are not always on our side when it comes to raising up young queens for God.

We must deal head-on with the images of females that are being lifted up in today's culture. While young people in general are affected by society's messages, girls in particular feel the impact. We must help them think more critically about the music they listen to and the movies and television shows they watch. That doesn't mean we should tell them what they should and shouldn't watch or listen to, but we should encourage them to think about what is really being said in a song or what ideas about women are being sold in an advertisement.

As a youth leader you might want to form small groups lead by adult women in which music or movie clips are used to open discussions about how women are portrayed by society and how that makes the girls feel. (Of course, use prayer and discretion when choosing music or movies to use.) Then leaders can point the girls to the stories of women who are lifted up in the Bible and compare them to what is being said by the music or movies. Another option would be to look at advertisements in magazines or commercials on television in which women are used to sell a product and talk about what message is being sent. This may even be a good discussion to have with the entire youth group so that the boys can share about how these advertisements affect the way they see girls. You might have an annual "Young Queens Retreat" in which you break the ice with fun activities like makeovers and then invite professional women to talk about college and careers or about the Proverbs 31 woman or Esther. It should be a time when women "keep it real" about issues of body image, sexuality and matters of the soul. Monthly small group meetings in which six to eight girls meet with adult women leaders for prayer, study and discussion can also equip them to figure out for themselves what it means to live life as queens of destiny.

Our girls are daily bombarded by our culture's messages of who they are. It is our responsibility to meet those messages head-on and show our girls their true images in the eyes of God. We can combat the negative images by exposing girls to both the biblical images of women leaders and strong Christian women right in their own church and community.

***Past actions.*** Our past and present actions often give power to the images we have of ourselves and the way others see us. At Patrick Henry, I saw that the girls' attitudes during a game would change based on their standing on the scoreboard. If they got behind, they started to act like losers before the game was even over, putting their heads down and fighting amongst themselves—and the other team saw this. In order to become winners, we had to change our attitudes and the way we acted on the court. We talked about how our attitudes affected how we were perceived by the opposing team as well as the crowd that was watching the game. We had to realize that our private practice affected our public game play.

The same is true of youth ministries that are focused on raising up young queens. We must deal head-on with how the girls in our youth ministries carry themselves. How do their attitudes and actions affect how they are perceived by others? Do they break negative stereotypes about females, or do they live up to them?

Again, this issue can be addressed in small-group or retreat settings in which girls are led by adult women. As our girls begin to realize just how much their actions and attitudes affect the way others see them, they can change those images. When they start acting like winners, they will be seen as winners—by others and by themselves.

***Religious sexism.*** At Patrick Henry High School I not only had to deal with how the other schools perceived our girls' team. I also had to deal with teachers and students within our own school who also saw our girls as losers. It's one thing to fight an enemy from without, but what about when the enemy is within?

The sad truth is that there is just as much sexism in the church—if not more at times—than in the secular world. I once saw a brochure for a youth ministry conference that offered a seminar designed especially for women; it focused on how to prepare meals and put on a banquet for one hundred or more people. What a limited view of women in ministry and God's call on their lives! Mike Yaconelli, cofounder of Youth Specialties, once said "that we spend so much time looking to fight the devil outside the church that we miss the devil that is sitting right there on the inside of the church."

In order to be effective in raising up young queens, we have to be honest about the sexism that lives within the church. We battle not just against secular forces but also against forces within our ministries that are contrary to God's image of girls and women. While Jesus was on earth, he radically changed how women were perceived in both the secular and the temple cultures. We get a feel for this radicalism in the story of a Canaanite woman who approached Jesus to ask him to heal her daughter:

> A Canaanite woman from that vicinity came to him, crying out, "Lord, Son of David, have mercy on me! My daughter is suffering terribly from demon-possession."
>
> Jesus did not answer a word. So his disciples came to him and urged him, "Send her away, for she keeps crying out after us."
>
> He answered, "I was sent only to the lost sheep of Israel."
>
> The woman came and knelt before him. "Lord, help me!" she said.
>
> He replied, "It is not right to take the children's bread and toss it to their dogs."
>
> "Yes, Lord," she said, "but even the dogs eat the crumbs that fall from their masters' table."
>
> Then Jesus answered, "Woman, you have great faith! Your request is granted." And her daughter was healed from that very hour. (Matthew 15:22-28)

In the culture this woman lived in, women were considered second-class citizens. She was not supposed to come into a room full of men and demand attention, yet there she was, crying out to Jesus for the healing of her daughter. The disciples responded to her in the way most people in that culture would have: They wanted to send her away. Yet Jesus made a counter-cultural move and honored the woman's faith. And this was not the only time when Jesus spoke out against the second-class citizenship of women. He sat at the well and brought transformation to the life of a Samaritan woman (see John 4:1-26). He allowed a prostitute to gain dignity by allowing her to prepare him for burial (Matthew 26:6-13). He healed a diseased and outcast woman (Matthew 9:20-22). Jesus brought revolutionary change to his society and the way it perceived women.

Are we (the church) in any way an obstacle to God's mission for girls and women? Have we fed into the negative images and stereotypes in our culture and allowed them to shape the way we perceive women? We must look within as well as without in our battle against the false perceptions that hinder our girls from fulfilling their God-intended destinies. We cannot afford to let mere misinterpretations of Scripture become an obstacle to helping girls truly understand who they are. The Bible actually gives a much broader picture of women than both the church as a whole and secular society. Don't let one line in the Bible about women being silent keep you from seeing the larger theme of women as teachers, prophets, ministers and executive leaders at the highest levels of office. Although there are instances in the Bible of women as concubines and victims of rape, and instructions for women not to teach men, do these images show us in totality how God views women? My answer is no, because we must take into consideration other biblical images of women. For example, Anna is mentioned in the second chapter of Luke (vv. 36-38) as a prophetess. It would be hard to remain silent in that role! I've already mentioned Esther, but let me add that her willingness to be a vocal queen saved the lives of her people. A whole book in the Old Testament is written in her name. Deborah is mentioned in Judges 4 as a prophetess who judged Israel. And Tabitha is referred to in Acts 9:36 as a disciple who helped the poor through kindness and charity. When we look at the Bible as a whole, it's clear that God doesn't view women as second-class citizens, so we the church can't afford in any manner to view girls that way.

## ON THE BATTLEFIELD FOR GIRLS

We are in a battle for our girls' lives. Even though we are fighting against the things in our culture that point girls away from who they really are in God, we must recognize that we are ultimately fighting a spiritual battle.

There are girls in our youth ministries who are dealing with serious issues, from body image to depression to the pressure to be "real" women and have sex. They are dealing with demonic forces dispatched into their lives to keep them from becoming young queens for God. Are we prepared to fight on behalf of these girls, or are we lost on what to do with them, like the disciples were with the boy plagued by seizures?

A few years before I began coaching at Patrick Henry, I was invited to speak at a weekend youth retreat for a local youth ministry in Minneapolis. After I had given my first message a girl came up to me for prayer and to find answers. After praying a general prayer over her that she would grow in her relationship with God, I asked her what she was seeking an answer to.

She lifted up her shirt sleeve and showed me where she had cut words like *hope* and *love* into her arms with a razor blade. They were scabbed over with her own dried blood.

I looked with shock at the words on her arm, trying to act calm even though this was the first time I had encountered a "cutter." "I want to know how to stop doing this to myself," she said. I wondered if the disciples felt the same way I did just then when the boy with seizures was brought to them. I was at a loss for words.

### MINISTRY MODEL

Jesus understood that there were demonic forces that sought to keep young people from becoming what they were created to be. He went to war against demons in order to holistically liberate young people:

> When they came to the crowd, a man approached Jesus and knelt before him. "Lord, have mercy on my son," he said. "He has seizures and is suffering greatly. He often falls into the fire or into the water. I brought him to your disciples, but they could not heal him."
>
> "O unbelieving and perverse generation," Jesus replied, "how long shall I stay with you? How long shall I put up with you? Bring the boy here to me." Jesus rebuked the demon, and it came out of the boy, and he was healed from that moment.
>
> Then the disciples came to Jesus in private and asked, "Why couldn't we drive it out?"
>
> He replied, "Because you have so little faith." (Matthew 17:14-20)

Finally I asked her why she was doing this to herself, and she said the pain of cutting herself helped her deal with the pain she was going through in life, including her parents' divorce and breaking up with her boyfriend. I invited one of the adult women leaders to come over and join me, and we listened to the girl's stories and prayed for her. I felt a spiritual war going on in that room, and I must admit that my faith was rocked that night. But, just like with the disciples, Jesus was there with me, and as we prayed I felt the presence of God move in that room as well.

There are many experts and teachers in youth ministry who don't want to touch the idea of spiritual warfare, and that's very unfortunate. I know that talking about these kinds of issues isn't easy, and I realize that there are some who have abused the concept. Could it be, however, that even this is a scheme of the enemy to keep us from truly understanding the battle that we are in? We cannot shy away from the need for a warfare approach in youth ministry in order to raise up young heroes for God.

## IN THE FOOTSTEPS OF ESTHER

I love reading the story of Esther in the Bible because it's about a young woman who was raised up as a queen despite her second-class status in terms of social rank and gender. In fact, today she would be considered a foster child. Yet Esther became a queen — and not just a prom queen in a fancy dress. She was queen of a whole nation, and she brought political, social and spiritual change to her land. Esther serves as a perfect model for our young women today. I have seen firsthand how her story can change the way that girls see themselves.

During my first year as coach of the girls' basketball team at Patrick Henry High School, I began to see a real turnaround. With the support of my staff, I had tried to help the girls see themselves as winners. We had high expectations for them, and we were starting to see it pay off. We weren't winning every game, but we were winning more than we were losing. In fact, by February we had won all of our conference games and had only lost three nonconference games. Even though I tried not to put too much pressure on the girls, I was excited for the first week of February, because it was then that we were scheduled to play Minneapolis North, the team that had beaten us 120-26 two seasons before. I had been thinking about that game all year.

On the night of our game against Minneapolis North, I could hear the girls in their team locker room getting ready with their usual pregame ritual of talking loudly and blasting rap music on a boom box. Normally I didn't mind their routine, but that night the music they were listening to kept using the "B" word over and over again. Now, I like rap music in general, but I can't stand songs that degrade women. I sent my female assistant coach into the girls' locker room to tell them to turn off that music.

When I met the girls downstairs for a pep talk before the game, I forgot that I was supposed to be their basketball coach and became a youth pastor right in front of their eyes. "Why do you listen to music that calls you a b——?" I asked. "You are not a b——! This is not where you should find your identity and purpose. Haven't you read the book of Esther? If you had you would know that you are queens! You are young women of destiny and purpose. It doesn't matter your home situation tonight. It doesn't matter your skin color tonight. It doesn't matter what certain rap songs or other people call you. You are queens! Do you understand who you are? You are queens! Now get up there and win that game!" Not bad for a spontaneous pregame pep talk!

We lost that game by seventeen points, which I guess was an improvement since we didn't lose by one hundred, but we lost all the same. Afterward I was sitting in my office trying to deal with the defeat when one of my players, Shauntel, walked in. She was crying, and I figured that it was because we had just lost the game. But then she said, "I just wanted to say thanks for calling me a queen. No one has ever called me a queen before. I just wanted to say thank you."

That night I was reminded of my duty to serve as an undercover youth minister while coaching that team, reminding urban girls who they really were in God's eyes. The story of Esther is proof that God can take a young woman, no matter her circumstances, and raise her up to be a queen. The stories of some of the girls from the Patrick Henry basketball team who went on to finish college are proof that girls like them can live up to their full potential if they begin to see themselves through God's eyes. As youth leaders, we must help girls understand this. Even if they've never known their biological parents, they can become queens. No matter what their ethnicity is, they can become queens. No matter what they've done in the past, it's not too late to say, "I desire to become a queen for God."

## RAISING YOUNG QUEENS

We need women in our youth ministries who will be loving mentors to girls and at the same time work to break the false perceptions of women that may exist among the boys in the youth ministry as well as others both in the church and the secular world. There is also a need for Christian men speaking God's truth into the lives of girls. For some girls, a youth minister or volunteer adult may be the only male voice speaking God's truth into their lives.

God is in the business of raising up young queens. Within our youth ministries we must develop ministry models specifically designed to reach out to our girls. They must hear stories about women in the Bible like Esther and Deborah (see Judges 4). They must see that God used girls and women in the Bible in incredible ways and that they can be used in the same way today. We must speak truth, encouragement and empowerment into their lives so that they can rise above negative images and stereotypes. We must remind them of their true destinies as young queens in the eyes of God.

# 6

## LEADERSHIP
### DEVELOPING YOUNG LEADERS FOR GOD

*Josiah was eight years old when he became king, and . . . he did*

*what was right in the eyes of the LORD. (2 Kings 22:1-2)*

We've already seen that the Bible is full of stories about God using young people to do revolutionary things. One of those young people is Josiah, who became king when he was eight years old. During his reign he discovered the power of the Word of God, known at the time as the Book of the Law. When he realized that his people had strayed from God's direction, he actually tore his robes. Then he brought about revolutionary change within his nation because of his encounter with the Word of God (see 2 Kings 22:11-13; 23:1-3).

God didn't believe that Josiah was too young to become a king, and when Josiah heard the words of the Book of the Law, he was moved in such a way that he was changed as an individual and as a leader, which in turn led to the transformation of a nation. Could it be that through the Word of God young people really get a glimpse of who they are and what they can become? Could it be that if young people today were to connect to stories like this they too could bring about transformation? Could families, neighborhoods and schools be transformed because of youth who are inspired by Josiah and other young revolutionaries?

I believe the answer is yes. There is something powerful about the Bible, the authoritative Word of God. It can bring light, liberation, identity and direction to the young people who find within its pages examples of other youth who changed the world. As youth leaders we must help young people to see themselves as potential heroes for God by presenting the Bible to them in a way that transforms the way they think, talk and live.

## TEACHING THEM THE WORD

It is ultimately God who transforms lives, but through the reading, understanding and applying of the Scriptures, students are brought into God's presence where he can begin his work. As leaders, we must help youth encounter the Bible at a level they can understand, but without watering down the authentic truth of the Word of God. We can start by helping them see themselves in the stories of young people who were just like them. Point them to the stories of youth like Esther and Timothy. Prove to them through the stories that no matter where they are in life, no matter how young they are, they can be used by God to make a difference.

Sometimes for young people Bible studies are boring and only about what they *can't* do. We must learn to present the stories we study in such a way that young people sense the excitement and drama of all that they *can* do. In the same way that they dream about becoming famous athletes or musicians, they should desire to be like the young heroes of the Bible.

As you're helping students identify with the stories in the Bible, keep in mind that you must be equipped to deal with ethnic diversity and to speak specifically to the challenges that at-risk youth from inner-city neighborhoods deal with. If you are in a situation in which you are working with multiethnic, urban youth, a Bible that portrays all white characters doesn't work—and it wouldn't even be accurate. The Bible is the most multiethnic piece of literature you'll ever put your hands on, and we do the Scriptures a disservice when we fail to recognize the diversity that is apparent in its pages. If you learn to present the Bible stories in a way that reflects the diversity of their characters, you will be equipped to show all students, regardless of their background or ethnicity, that they can be used by God to do extraordinary things.

Theater and drama can be a great way to get young people involved in the Bible in a deeper way. I was a theater major in college, and the experience of acting in plays was a great way to get in touch not only with the various characters that I played but also with the setting and culture in which the play took place, as well as the intention of the writer.

One way to use drama would be to break up your youth group into small groups, give each group a Bible story that centers around a young person and then have them act it out as a skit. You could go even deeper after the skit by having the person who played the main character stay in character and answer other questions about their life. If you have young people in the youth group who really have a heart for theater you could take more time over some months to actually write a one-act play based on Scripture, develop a cast and perform it in front of the whole church.

In the age of *The Message* it might be fitting for your youth group to use forms like poetry and rap to paraphrase the Bible and break it down into the language of students' culture. Rap, spoken word and theater are all tools that can be used to study and bring the Word of God to life.

## WHEN YOUTH LEAD

The Word of God caused Josiah to act. In the same way, Bible study should call us to action. We should point our young people toward the Bible not so that they can learn a whole lot of facts and information, but so that they can be developed into leaders who take the gospel message to those in their circles of influence.

Youth groups can take missions trips each year to diverse places like New York, Jamaica and Mexico. Students can contribute to worship through drama, dance teams and worship bands. They can be involved in planning, drama, dance, music and speaking.

Making this transition to youth-led groups who care about outreach begins with studying God's Word together. In Ginghamsburg we began creating a holistic model of youth leadership development by exploring what the Bible says about raising up young heroes for God. And, it is interesting to note that the youth ministry's tremendous hunger for missions and outreach began years before I arrived there with a Bible study led by the previous youth pastor. It's one thing to study the Bible from the standpoint of laws or dos and don'ts. It's another thing altogether to view and study the Bible as a call to action by leading and serving.

**MINISTRY MODEL**

At Ginghamsburg United Methodist Church in Tipp City, Ohio, the youth ministry got involved in community leadership and birthed a nonprofit foundation called Dream Builders. One of the foundation's programs, Clubhouse, sends the youth group into the inner city of Dayton to run tutoring programs and Bible clubs. The program is mainly student-led, with adults acting as trainers and mentors, and its impact reaches beyond just the city of Dayton. It touches other areas of southern Ohio, and there have even been young people who have graduated and gone on to start Clubhouse programs in Illinois and North Carolina.

## LETTING THE YOUTH TAKE OVER

The key to a youth ministry that actively moves on the Word of God is in having an environment in which leadership from young people is affirmed. Youth leaders may say they want youth to take leadership, but when they see it in action they often have a different feeling.

About four years ago I had the chance to speak to a group of youth at a camp in Arizona. When I gave the altar call on the second night, a girl named Crystal came forward. I prayed for her and then I moved on to pray for other young people. Meanwhile, Crystal remained at the altar praying, singing and laughing out loud. The adult leaders and I were watching her, wondering what she was doing. Even as I finished with the altar call and gave the closing prayer, she stayed at the altar. Then she looked at me and said, "Now I know what I'm really supposed to do with my life." She began to walk over to other young people and pray for them. Those she prayed for began to cry and sing, and some just fell on their knees and lifted their hands to God.

One of the adult leaders announced through the microphone that the service was officially over and that it was time to prepare for some icebreakers and other events, but even as people began to leave, Crystal stayed behind, still praying for a group of the youth. Together they were singing, praying and lifting their hands to God. I could tell that some of the adults were beginning to be bothered by Crystal because she was not being obedient to the orders that had just been given. One of them approached the group and told them to break it up and prepare for the icebreakers.

Later that night as I was standing in line in the cafeteria, I noticed a table of young people with their Bibles open and their heads down in prayer—and there was Crystal, sitting among them and ministering to them. It was then that I realized that the adults in our group (myself included) had been standing in the way of God using young people to advance his kingdom. That week God had intended to use Crystal to minister in a powerful way to her peers, and the adults, worried about our own plans, had tried to get in the way.

If we are to witness God's hand moving through the lives of our students, we must create environments in which their leadership is affirmed and supported. We must keep our eyes open and be ready for God to change our plans at any moment. We may just find that God's new plan, which had seemed to thwart ours, is actually an answer to our prayers!

In addition, we should realize that if we don't take into account the importance of leadership development and work to empower our young people in holistic, biblical ways, their leadership skills may end up being developed under negative influences. A lot of kids who sell drugs, lead gangs and throw forbidden parties are able to successfully do these things because of their God-given leadership skills. If we don't proactively develop young leaders in ways that are positive and productive, their skills could develop in ways that take them far away from God's plan for their lives.

**MINISTRY MODEL**

Even churches that can't afford full-time youth ministers can find ways to empower their students to take on leadership roles. The Urban Leadership Academy in the Twin Cities Metro Area is a faith-based organization headed by a pastor named Darrell Geddes that every summer pulls young people from churches all over the city to help them develop their leadership skills. Then it sends them back to their churches in the fall along with adult mentors and encourages them to bring transformation to their local churches and surrounding neighborhoods. Youth go back to their churches equipped to assist volunteer and part-time adult youth leaders in all aspects of ministry, from Sunday school to planning midweek gatherings to other special events. The young people learn to use their unique gifts to develop a stronger youth ministry in their local church.

## THE REVOLUTION

God has a mission for young people, and we should not hinder him. There is a place for young people up close to God. Take the time to survey the youth in your ministry. What untapped gifts of leadership are right there in front of you that could advance God's kingdom in powerful ways? In what ways can you equip your youth to use those gifts for God's glory?

The Bible is full of revolutionary stories with young people at the center of them. In these stories young people take on giants, challenge kings, proclaim the words of God and develop churches. What powerful stories are ready to be developed within the youth in your ministry? The Bible can be a powerful springboard to move from God stories of the past to God stories in the present and future. The revolution begins when the power and actions read about in the Bible take up residence in the youth around you. Gather the young people, open the Bible, give them leadership skills and let the revolution begin.

# 7

## MULTIETHNIC

### THE HIP-HOP INFLUENCE ON YOUTH CULTURE

A few months ago I was speaking to an all-white class of seminary students in Minnesota. At the end of my presentation, one young man asked me a question that went something like this: "I'm a youth pastor in a rural area in an all-white church, but there is a growing Asian and Hispanic youth population that has migrated to my town, and I don't know how to reach them. There are also some multiracial families that are now in the town as well. How do I reach young people in the age of the Tiger Woods and Mariah Carey youth culture?"

In today's world there is a growing multiethnic society, and it is having an influence on our young people. A May 2000 *Newsweek* article reports the following:

> Thirty years ago, only one in every 100 children born in the United States was of mixed race. Today that number is one in 19. In states like California and Washington it's closer to one in 10. The morphing demographics give many teens a chance to challenge old notions of race. (Lynette Clemetson, "Color My World," *Newsweek*, May 8, 2000)

We can see evidence of this multiethnic trend by looking to the media. Mountain Dew commercials feature African American, Asian American and European American youth riding dirt bikes and drinking Mountain Dew. Barbie commercials feature multiethnic girls playing with multiethnic dolls. Gap commercials feature a multiethnic cast of characters dancing, singing and skating together in Gap jeans.

This growing multiracial population has been and will continue to radically tear down the walls of race and culture that separated previous generations. Yet even though youth are being influenced by a multiethnic society, they usually walk into homogenous youth groups in which leaders seem unaware of the coming multicultural youth revolution and the influence it's already having on young people.

## THE HIP-HOP INFLUENCE

I grew up in the '80s in an urban area of South Minneapolis in an African American, middle-class home, and I was definitely interested in things that were considered a part of "black culture" at the time. I was very much into rap music (groups like Run-DMC, Public Enemy, Eric B. and Rakim) and basketball (though my court skills were nothing to brag about), and I had a number of black friends. However, during that time in my life I was primarily influenced by teenagers who lived in a different part of the city and were very different from me. For three of my teenage years my clothing, speech and choice of music were influenced by a group of white teens from an affluent part of town. Maybe it was because I thought they had a better life than me. Maybe it was because a lot of the television shows I watched featured mostly white characters and this group seemed a lot like the characters I admired. Whatever the reason, if they had skateboards, I wanted one. I wanted penny loafers, because that was what they wore. I listened to music by Kansas, Hall and Oates, and the Police (I hope you realize how hard it is for an urban African American to admit to this!) because that was the music I heard when I visited the homes of those kids.

It is likely that other black teenagers were influenced by white culture in the same ways that I was. Today, however, that trend has reversed itself. Urban, hip-hop, "black" youth culture now has an influence on society as a whole. Many white teens living far from the streets of the inner city are influenced by the slang, fashion and music of the 'hood. I've even read in quite a few articles that if white suburban teens stopped buying rap music, the genre would go out of business.

In his book *Hip Hop America* Nelson George talks about the influence of hip-hop music on American society:

Now we know that rap music, and hip hop style as a whole, has utterly broken through from its ghetto roots to assert a lasting influence on American clothing, magazine publishing, television, language, sexuality, and social policy as well as its obvious presence in records and movies. . . . Advertisers, magazines, MTV, fashion companies, beer and soft drink manufacturers, and multimedia conglomerates like Time-Warner have embraced hip hop as a way to reach not just black young people but all young people. (Introduction, ix)

I have had the opportunity to witness this firsthand during my time as a youth pastor at Ginghamsburg United Methodist Church in Tipp City, Ohio. When I arrived at this predominately white and suburban/rural megachurch, I was nervous. The youth group had around two hundred young people, and at least 99.99 percent of them were white, suburban and rural. I kept asking myself, "How in the world am I going to be able to identify with these young people? I have nothing in common with them. They're white and I'm black. They're from the suburbs and I'm from the city. Why in the world did this church hire an urban youth worker to fill this position?" For the first month or so I was burdened with questions like these. But then I began to notice a few things that changed how I felt.

One weekend I went to a football game at the local high school and, sure enough, I stuck out in the crowd. Some people asked me if I was Emmit Smith (the Dallas Cowboys football player) or Will Smith (no explanation needed), but I responded with the truth that I was actually Efrem Smith. The fact that I was mistaken for these famous African American men was my first hint that the black culture was having an influence, even on people in Tipp City, Ohio.

After the game, as I was getting into my car, two white teenage boys were getting into their pickup truck, which was parked next to me. One of the boys had on a baseball cap, the other a cowboy hat. The truck had two confederate flag stickers in the back window and a gun rack, and I have to admit that I immediately began to stereotype the teens right there in the parking lot. But then something happened that shocked me and changed the way I look at the youth culture of today. The teens started up the truck and rolled down their windows, blasting Snoop Dogg (a black rapper) on their stereo! Then they looked at me and said, "What's up, dawg?" before driving away, leaving me stunned.

Early on I connected with some of the boys through video game tournaments, which were held in the bedroom of whoever was hosting each week, and another thing I began to notice was that many of the white boys in that suburban community had posters of black athletes and rappers on their walls. In fact, one week during a Sunday school class I passed out a survey in order to get to know the youth better and learned that hip-hop was the favorite music genre of most of the students in the youth group. Although many of them admitted that I was the first black person they had ever developed a personal relationship with (in some cases, I was the first black person who had even entered their houses), they were being influenced by a black and urban culture long before they met me.

As I spent time with the youth in my new ministry, I began to recognize how well I was connecting with the young people. Even though I was from the city and they were not, just by being myself I was connecting with many of them. I didn't have to change my slang, favorite music or fashion, because they could already identify with my urban roots.

Whether you've taken the time to notice it or not, many youth, regardless of their ethnicity or where they live, are influenced by the urban youth culture. And if all this is true, then we must change the way we approach youth ministry. We can no longer minister to our young people without considering the things that influence them, hip-hop culture included.

## GANGSTA RAP CULTURE

Gangsta rap, which is characterized by explicit lyrics that degrade women and talk about gangs, drugs and violence, is one aspect of hip-hop culture that has gained more media attention than others, and it is having a definite impact on our society.

Two of the biggest rappers in mainstream hip-hop culture today are Eminem and 50 Cent, both of whom have street credibility (which seems to be important to many young people these days) because they claim to have lived out most of what they are rapping about. Eminem raps about his dysfunctional mother, his drug use and his fantasies of killing his "baby's momma." 50 Cent claims to have real bullets in his body and to have sold drugs and beaten people down. And should I even bring up Tupac Shakur? Many people believe that he is dead, but whether he is or not, he is still prominent in gangsta culture. He was shot, spent time in jail for raping a girl and is associated with the ultimate gangsta music label, Death Row Records. Even after his alleged death, his label has continued to release new Tupac albums, which have topped the charts in sales.

Rappers like Eminem, 50 Cent and Tupac are clearly in positions of influence, and not only with the inner-city youth culture; they actually stay in business by attracting a strong following amongst white, suburban youth. Unfortunately, urban African American youth have often been stereotyped by people who think gangsta rap and the values it promotes are all that hip-hop and African American culture is about. Even more unfortunately, some of the youth who are influenced by this kind of music embrace the gangsta lifestyle they hear about and see through the influence of these artists.

Gangsta rap has been largely responsible for the glamorization of the thug, the bad guy who is really a good guy. There is evidence of this trend all around us in pop culture. In today's movies and television shows, we see thugs who cheat, exploit and kill yet are caring and sensitive beneath their tough exteriors. Just watch *The Sopranos* to see what I mean. Or *The Godfather* trilogy, *The King of New York*, *The Warriors*, *The Mack* or *Scarface*, just to name a few.

Or take for example professional wrestling. When I watched it as a kid, it was always easy to tell the good guy from the bad guy. The good guy wore light colors and was kind and friendly to the crowd, while the bad guy wore dark colors and was angry and mean. Today, however, the distinctions have been blurred. Now when a guy comes into the ring, shouting and giving the crowd the finger, smashing beer cans on his head, the crowd cheers because he's the good guy. The bad guy, the thug, has been morphed into a superhero. We even see this in the arena of true professional sports (lest you think I believe professional wrestling is a true sport) in the characters of thug athletes like Dennis Rodman or Bill Laimbeer, formerly of the Detroit Pistons.

The point I'm trying to make here is that what I like to call "thugology" is all around us. It's in movies, music, sports and yes, even politics, and it does have an influence on our young people. So what do we as Christians do to address it? Do we create youth ministries that shelter young people from the "real" world? No. Instead we must simply follow the ministry methods of Jesus. Instead of focusing on sheltering the "good" people, he targeted thugs in his ministry.

They went across the lake to the region of the Gerasenes. When Jesus got out of the boat, a man with an evil spirit came from the tombs to meet him. This man lived in the tombs, and no one could bind him any more, not even with a chain. For he had often been chained hand and foot, but he tore the chains apart and broke the irons on his feet. No one was strong enough to subdue him. Night and day among the tombs and in the hills he would cry out and cut himself with stones.

When he saw Jesus from a distance, he ran and fell on his knees in front of him. (Mark 5:1-6)

Then it happened that as Jesus was reclining at the table in the house, behold, many tax collectors and sinners came and were dining with Jesus and His disciples. When the Pharisees saw this, they said to His disciples, "Why is your Teacher eating with the tax collectors and sinners?" (Matthew 9:10-11 NASB)

Jesus was accused by religious leaders of hanging out with the wrong people. But these sinners were exactly the ones Jesus centered his earthly ministry around. Even on the cross Jesus took the time to bring a criminal into heaven. In John 4 Jesus went out of his way to go to Samaria, a town of outcasts, and minister to a woman at the well. Jesus sought out the thugs of his day and offered them love, grace and, most importantly, transformation. He cared about the outcast, the gangsta, the "playa." He didn't ignore them or condemn them; instead he healed them of the internal hurts and pains that were oppressing their spirits. He created a refuge for them and gave them a chance to experience his love. Jesus didn't run from thugs; they ran to him, and in turn he transformed their lives. In this same spirit, we must make outreach to the thug, the at-risk and the outcast a part of our ministry to youth.

You can't deny the influence of thug and gangsta culture on the young people around you. Even if you're not in inner-city ministry, this issue still affects the youth you work with. In today's society there is a need for youth ministry professionals who know enough about hip-hop and urban culture to know what gangsta rap is and the influence it has. We must also know that there is more to hip-hop culture than the thugs, and we must develop ministries that are geared specifically toward today's urban-influenced youth culture.

## AN OUTCAST MINISTRY

If it's true that the youth culture has become more multicultural and urban-influenced, then why does mainstream youth ministry still come across as so male, suburban and white in its leadership, marketing, training and practical theology? Youth ministry speakers, leaders and professors seem to care very little about putting urban or multiethnic issues at the forefront of their agendas. Perhaps this is because there aren't many full-time urban youth pastors, or maybe it's because youth ministry has become big business and the money that keeps it big business comes from outside at-risk communities.

I am concerned that even though today's youth cross racial and ethnic lines more proactively than any generation has before them, most adult youth ministry leaders seem to be satisfied with presenting a suburban, white youth ministry model that focuses more on game ideas than talking about what's really influencing youth today. No one seems to want to deal with why the pain, hopelessness and anger of the youth of the city have now found a home in rural areas through school shootings all across the country. No one really wants to talk about how racism has kept us from really developing a radical and revolutionary global model for youth ministry that could raise a generation of young people to build the authentic, Christ-centered and multiethnic church that is described in Acts 2:42-47.

We can no longer afford to treat urban youth ministry as a misfit, outcast ministry. The new, radical voice of youth ministry comes from the 'hood. Gangsta rap and hip-hop culture aren't influencing just the hearts and minds of urban youth. Those voices have found their way into the souls of the youth culture as a whole. Yet many youth ministry leaders have decided to live in denial, just like many white suburban parents pretend their kids aren't making decisions based on the lyrics of rap songs. We must take the time to pay attention and catch up with reality. We cannot prepare youth to be kingdom-builders within the world in which they live if the world *we* live in seems like another planet to them.

The best way for youth leaders to catch up with the times is to build hip-hop culture and multiethnic issues into the framework of our youth ministries. This begins with us. We cannot take young people where we are not willing to go. We must be willing to immerse ourselves in understanding hip-hop, urban and multiethnic cultures. We can do this by diversifying the types of books we read and the movies we watch. As we live in the reality of this urban, multiethnic culture, we will be better equipped not only to reach youth within the cultures they live, but also to empower them as kingdom-builders.

## MINISTERING TO YOUTH IN A MULTIETHNIC SOCIETY

Just as intimacy with God is important for raising up young heroes, so is equipping young people to minister within the diverse, urban and hip-hop-influenced culture in which they live. Start by asking yourself some important questions: "Could the kids in my youth group bring their unchurched friends to this youth ministry, even those who are of a different ethnic background?" "Does this youth ministry reach out to *all* of the youth in the surrounding area?" If the answer is "no," then begin your exploration into a multiethnic approach to youth ministry by taking your students to visit a church that is primarily of a different ethnicity than yours. Plan an event, such as a missions trip, and invite the youth group from that church to participate.

As you begin to explore and understand other cultures, there are three things your youth ministry—both you and the young people you work with—must understand in order to be radical reconcilers in this multiethnic world.

*The Bible is multiethnic.* As we've already discussed, the Bible is the most multiethnic piece of literature you will ever put your hands on. It is full of stories of diversity. Take, for example, the story in Acts 2 in which the Holy Spirit came upon the apostles in the midst of a multiethnic, Jewish crowd. Peter preached to that crowd, and three thousand people received the message. Their lives were totally transformed, and they came together to build the first Christian church through worship, teaching, serving and sharing meals together. From this point the book of Acts moves to expand the community of God beyond just the Jewish people to include the Gentiles as well. Unfortunately, the Bible is rarely presented as the diverse book that it is. Often it is presented as a story about white people, and this segregated depiction cheapens the gospel. We must present the authentic, multiethnic story of the Bible to our young people. When they realize that the Bible applies to people of all ethnicities, not only will the stories come alive to them; they will also be more equipped to minister to those around them.

*Jesus was multiethnic.* We are instructed to worship God in spirit and in truth (see John 4:23-24). To worship God in spirit is to know him outside of the natural realm, but we must also worship him in truth, which means having a true and realistic perception of both who he is supernaturally and who he was on earth.

In the second chapter of the Gospel of Matthew, the writer records an event in the life of Jesus that sheds some light on the physical appearance of Jesus and his family. Joseph, Mary, and the infant Jesus fled Palestine into Egypt to escape the death threats of Herod. . . . For Jesus and his family to blend in with African people, their appearance must have been quite similar to that of the people living in Egypt at the time. . . . Jesus no doubt had a distinct Asian-ness and African-ness about his culture and probably his physical features. . . . We can only reconfirm our earlier contention that Jesus, like other Jews in Palestine who had descended from the Hebrew people, was Afro-Asiatic. (From *Coming Together: The Bible's Message in an Age of Diversity* by Curtiss Paul DeYoung)

Jesus' genealogy indicates that he was not white, not African, but multiethnic (see Matthew 1:1-17). The multiethnicity that DeYoung speaks about centers around the African, Asian and Jewish (or Hebraic) roots within the earthly heritage of Jesus. There are some who say that it doesn't matter what color Jesus' skin was while he was here on earth. I believe, however, that it is important to understand that Jesus was multiethnic. A multiethnic Jesus represents all of humanity, not one particular race, and thus can bring about redemption, reconciliation and unity for a scattered humanity. In an increasingly multiethnic world a strictly white, black, red or yellow Jesus cannot accomplish the same widespread healing work of the multiethnic Jesus. By promoting and accepting an all-white image of Jesus, angels and other Bible characters, then, do we hinder our evangelism efforts? A segregated, homogenous church does not have the same potential power to reach others as does a Christ-centered, multiethnic church. If Jesus truly was multiethnic in human form, we are obligated to pass on authentic biblical truth to young people at a time when multiethnicity is valued more than it's ever been.

***Creation is multiethnic.*** Nowhere in the Scriptures would you be able to find a passage that says, "God made humans after their own kinds; black, white, red and yellow God made them. God made blacks after their own kind to live in their own unique way. God made whites after their own kind in their own unique way. And he made whites superior over all the other kinds of humans, because his true son, Jesus, would one day come to earth as a white man." The race system that exists today is not in place by the hand of God. In Genesis 1 and 2 we can see clearly that he created one unified humanity to dwell on his earth.

We all come from the same family, made by the same Creator, and it is important that Christians allow the Spirit of God to renew their minds and dismantle race-based systems within the church. This does not mean we should erase ethnicity and the various aspects of our cultures that define us as people. Exploring and appreciating diversity within the body of Christ is a vehicle to a greater understanding of the fullness of God. However, we must tear down the walls that separate us and move toward a church that values the multiethnic culture that it is a part of.

The fact that we live in a multiethnic, urban and hip-hop influenced youth culture is not something that should intimidate us or that we should be in denial about. Instead, we should embrace this opportunity for ministry like never before. We serve a Messiah who walked the earth as a multiethnic human being, and we lift up the Bible—the most multiethnic piece of literature we could ever put our hands on—as our authority. The challenge now is to create a ministry model within your ministry that has the ability to reach a hip-hop and urban influenced culture.

At the church I now pastor, called The Sanctuary Covenant

Church, we are attempting to do just that. Our church is committed to being a multiethnic and Christ-centered community that provides a relevant worship experience by using elements of hip-hop culture to reach the emerging generation and lift our praises up to God. We've invited Christian rap groups in our local area to come and lead us in worship. Our own praise and worship team has used rap, dance and spoken word within our services. Our ministries ought to give the hip-hop community within our local area the opportunity to use their gifts to glorify God and reach an unchurched people-group that traditional methods of ministry cannot. For example, there is a teenager named Eric in our church who is always in the front row excited about church. The main reason he is so enthusiastic about worship every week is because he knows he has the freedom to worship God using the elements of hip-hop he grew up in. One Sunday morning I brought him up front and asked him to dance and rap about God. Ever since, he's been in the front row, excited about God. Similarly, a friend of mine named Phil Jackson has started a new hip-hop church called The House that is reaching youth and young adults in the Lawndale community of Chicago. Using the hip-hop elements of the DJ, break dancing, rap and visual arts, Pastor Jackson attracted over five hundred people at their first service!

The church today should not run from the major influencers of the youth culture but instead use them to advance God's kingdom.

# 8

# SERVING
## NURTURING YOUNG KINGDOM-BUILDERS

*The word of the LORD came to me, saying,*

*"Before I formed you in the womb I knew you, before you were born I set you apart; I appointed you as a prophet to the nations."*

*"Ah, Sovereign LORD," I said, "I do not know how to speak; I am only a child."*

*But the LORD said to me, "Do not say, 'I am only a child.' You must go to everyone I send you to and say whatever I command you. Do not be afraid of them, for I am with you and will rescue you,"*

*declares the LORD. (Jeremiah 1:4-8)*

When I have implemented a revolutionary approach to youth ministry in the places where I have served as a youth leader, usually the first young people to respond are those who are very extroverted. When the challenge goes out to become young heroes for God through acts of service, these are the young people who move to the forefront of the youth ministry ready to lead a worship team, start a drama team, lead a Bible study at their high schools or do any number of other extroverted, up-front kinds of kingdom building. But not all young people feel confident that they can be heroes for God, that they can be used by him to do extraordinary things. Not all young people believe that they have the gifts, talents and abilities to build God's kingdom right now. There are various reasons why they feel this way, but for some of them it is simply because they don't possess the aggressive personalities that would place them in the forefront of Christian service.

## A BODY OF CHRIST ISSUE

This is more than a youth group issue. This is a body of Christ issue. Too often Christians are absent from the front lines of kingdom building because we put too much of our focus on the celebrity megachurch pastors and those who are dynamic and aggressive leaders. As a result of that focus, those who don't feel called to preach or lead feel like second-class citizens in the body of Christ and do little to further the kingdom. This trend is obvious in three arenas of the Christian community: Christian television, the parachurch and the megachurch.

*Christian television.* Most of what you see on Christian television is focused on what I call a celebrity pastor. I'm not against visionary, motivating pastors who have the ability to communicate beyond the limits of their local congregations. What I'm concerned about, however, is that the focus is so centered on these pastors that the people watching them are not getting a picture of the impact they could make in kingdom building beyond sending in financial support to the celebrity pastor and becoming a "partner" in the ministry. This kind of mass television communication doesn't develop the kingdom-building movement to its greatest potential. Christians need to see everyday, ordinary people—servants—doing extraordinary

things for God in the world. They need to see themselves, because let's be honest, when people see pastors on television,
they probably aren't thinking, "I could do that!" Getting more
people on the front lines of kingdom building is about giving
people a picture of the impact they could make on a level that
they feel is attainable and attractive.

*Parachurches.* In the parachurch movement the biggest issue is that of funding. I know from my experiences with the
Fellowship of Christian Athletes and the Park Avenue Foundation that funding is crucial in order to maintain a ministry. The
mindset often then becomes that people of significant resources are needed in order to build God's kingdom, and the
focus turns to attracting people of financial means to the ministry. In turn, a person who doesn't have a lot of money but has
a heart for the ministry may not feel as important or needed in
the ministry as the wealthy donor who is mentioned in an annual report or given recognition through some award at a fund-
raising banquet. In order to combat this focus on funding, we
must put as much value on volunteers as on wealthy donors.
Raising up people, in the long run, is more important than
raising dollars, and often more people means more dollars anyway. Putting emphasis on people first and money second cre-
ates an environment in which more people are working in the
harvest field toward a parachurch's purpose.

*Megachurches.* The megachurch movement can have the
same problems as Christian television. There is such a focus
on the celebrity pastor that at times we lose out on the opportunity to get more people on the front lines of kingdom building. Yes, we do need more pastors with out-of-the-box, vision-

ary leadership skills. And we need growing churches with the people and resources to transform communities locally and globally. But so often the "ordinary" people in the church feel incapable compared to the celebrity pastors and as a result are not out in the harvest field doing the work of the kingdom.

## ENCOURAGING THE "ORDINARY" PEOPLE

So what about those other types of youth in our ministries? What about the shy types, those who are less outgoing? What about those quiet youth who sometimes get overlooked? Because I'm an extrovert myself, if I'm not careful I can get drawn to others like me who seem to be the real go-getters in ministry and forget about those quiet young people who have just as much to give to building the kingdom of God in their own right.

Because shy and introverted people are less aggressive in using their gifts, we must give them the support they need to realize that they too can do big things in God's kingdom. To reach out to these quiet heroes we have to start by making sure that we are proactively encouraging and empowering them.

Take a look at Jeremiah 1. God starts by letting Jeremiah know just how special and important he is. He tells Jeremiah that he was set apart and appointed for a special purpose—a purpose that began before Jeremiah was even formed in the womb (see Jeremiah 1:5). We must take special care to let introverted, shy and quiet young people know that they are special, that there is a unique calling upon their lives and that they are not less important than their outgoing, extroverted peers. By reminding them that God's calling was on their lives before they were even formed in the womb, we can help them see their shyness not as a deficiency, but as an asset. Could it be that there is something God-ordained about being shy? Could it be that God has a unique ministry for those who are quicker to listen than to speak? I believe the answer to both of those questions is yes.

After encouragement comes empowerment. In an earlier chapter I talked about the importance of backing up good words with actions, and that is what empowerment is all about. God told Jeremiah that he would equip him for his appointment to become a prophet to the nation of Israel, and then he put words in Jeremiah's mouth so that he could fulfill his calling (see Jeremiah 1:7-10). We need to be willing to follow up our words of encouragement to students with actions that show them we meant what we said.

When I was at the Park Avenue Foundation I met a quiet young man named Bobby who had just turned eighteen and didn't think much of himself. Every week when I would meet with him he would give me an excuse why he couldn't turn his life around. He told me stories of not knowing his father and how that had affected his life. He told me stories of abuse from other relatives and the pain that caused him. I tried everything I could through encouraging words to let him know that it wasn't too late for him to make a positive difference in his life and the lives of those around him. He looked at me in disbelief and stated, "Man, I can't even get a job!" I tried again to encourage him, telling him that he had the gifts and abilities to get and keep a job; he only had to change his attitude. He then told me that he had an opportunity to interview for a job that week but had nothing to wear. I decided it was time to put my encouraging words into action.

"Get in my car," I said. I took Bobby to Men's Warehouse clothing store and had him fitted for clothes appropriate for a job interview.

As we left the store, Bobby looked at me and just asked, "Why?"

"Because I believe in you," I said. Like God's encouragement and empowerment of Jeremiah, encouraging words backed by action can make a difference in a young person's life.

## EMPOWERING THE WORKERS

Most youth ministries today are dealing with the subject of leadership, and although I agree that this is important, I believe that if we want to raise up young heroes for God we must grab hold of the concept of service. Not everyone is called to leadership, but everyone in the body of Christ can be a servant. As a matter of fact, Jesus clearly called for an army of servant-workers in the Bible:

> Jesus went through all the towns and villages, teaching in their synagogues, preaching the good news of the kingdom and healing every disease and sickness. When he saw the crowds, he had compassion on them, because they were harassed and helpless, like sheep without a shepherd. Then he said to his disciples, "The harvest is plentiful but the workers are few. Ask the Lord of the harvest, therefore, to send out workers into his harvest field." (Matthew 9:35-38)

Jesus didn't say the celebrity pastors were few. He didn't say the ordained were few. He didn't even say the leaders were few. He said the *workers* were few and then he encouraged the disciples to ask God to send out workers into the world to address those sheep that are lost and need an almighty Shepherd. As we look at the youth in our ministries, we should be praying to God that he would use us to raise up our young people as servants who are equipped to go out into the harvest field. Whether loud, quiet, urban, suburban, jocks, artists or rebels, they all have something that can be contributed to the kingdom-building effort. Can you imagine the impact the body of Christ would have on the world if everyone who called themselves Christian saw themselves as vitally important to kingdom-building work?

In the body of Christ we need a movement that reaches the person in the last pew of the church and lets him know that he is special and has something unique to give to kingdom building. Let me share three focus areas in which you can develop and implement a ministry model of service into your youth ministry.

*Loving servants.* Being a servant begins with love. It's knowing the extent of God's love for us (see John 3:16-17) and in return loving him with every part of who we are. Young people probably won't be interested in hearing about God's calling on their lives if they don't feel loved. Paul understood this when he wrote:

> If I speak in the tongues of men and of angels, but have not love, I am only a resounding gong or a clanging symbol. If

I have the gift of prophecy and can fathom all mysteries and all knowledge, and if I have a faith that can move mountains, but have not love, I am nothing. If I give all I possess to the poor and surrender my body to the flames, but have not love, I gain nothing. (1 Corinthians 13:1-3)

Do we give our young people a reason to be servants by showing them just how much God loves them? In order to be true kingdom-builders they must be in loving relationship with the King. To be ambassadors of reconciliation, they must be in intimate relationship with the Reconciler.

After loving our young people, we must talk with them about the importance of loving God in return. We live the way we do out of our love for him. We become servants for God because we love him with everything that we are. Our intimacy with him becomes the well from which this love springs forth.

*A life of service.* We must let young people know that the lives they lead are important, that the way they live should be an outpouring of their love for God. They also need to know that right where they are in life they can build God's kingdom. Implementing service as a key component of your youth ministry is about letting young people know that their lives can make a difference right now. Their love for sports, drama or music is a potential ministry platform. We must help them see that the gifts, joys and passions that they carry to school, to their friends' houses or to the mall could start a revolutionary ministry to the people around them.

*A legacy of service.* Usually when people think of a legacy they think of something that is only achieved when a person dies. But what about equipping young people to have living legacies right now? Missions and service trips are a great way to start. By going back to the same place on an annual basis, young people are able to see the impact they are leaving on a particular community. When I was on staff at Ginghamsburg United Methodist Church, I went on a missions trip to Mexico, and while I was there the director of the Tijuana Christian Mission showed me all the work the Ginghamsburg youth group had done over the years. They had left a legacy behind them.

## A QUIET REVOLUTION

What equipped Jeremiah to fulfill his call was his intimate, up-close relationship with God. Building God's kingdom begins with an intimate relationship with him, and because shy or introverted young people tend to be quiet anyway, they may even have an easier time catching the importance of intimacy with God. This is another area in which we can encourage them. We can help them to understand that they can be the starters of a quiet revolution through their commitment to quiet, powerful and intimate moments with God.

This kind of quiet revolution is something I had the pleasure of witnessing firsthand when I arrived at Patrick Henry High School in 1998. At the time Patrick Henry didn't have a very good reputation in the community. Most of the young people who attended the school were there because they had no choice. The parents in that school district who were able to send their children to other schools made arrangements to do so. Just months into my time there I found out why Patrick Henry had the reputation it did.

At the time my job title was urban director for the Minnesota Fellowship of Christian Athletes. Because I wasn't a teacher in the building, the best time for me to see most of the players on my team was during the lunch hour, so I tried to get up to the school for lunch at least twice a week. During many of those lunchroom visits I witnessed fights in the halls and in the lunchroom, but after my second month there something much worse happened. A sophomore girl was shot and killed one day after school when her ex-boyfriend tried to impress her and win her back by showing off his uncle's gun. Just as we were recovering from that tragedy, another incident happened that hit a little closer to home for those of us on the basketball team. There was a senior boy who had transferred to our school from Ohio. I hadn't met him yet but kept hearing what a good student he was, what a great attitude he had and what every basketball coach wants to hear: that he was 6'8"! I was looking forward to meeting him at an open gym time after school that day, but while he was on the way back to school after going home to change his clothes, he confronted someone he had caught earlier in the week trying to break into his mother's car. The person he confronted had a gun and shot him in the head. He died instantly. In just a matter of months, two students' lives had been taken, and even though neither incident happened on school grounds, it only furthered Patrick Henry's reputation as the worst high school in Minneapolis.

It was during that difficult time at Patrick Henry that two quiet Christian students decided to respond. Their names were Grayson and Angie. They weren't the most extroverted students. They were also in the minority at the high school, since they were white and the school was predominantly black. But these two quiet students responded to the tragedies by simply going down to the gym lobby of the school a couple of times a week, sitting on the floor and praying for the school. They did this for weeks. They didn't preach; they didn't sing songs; they didn't parade down the halls with Bibles. They simply and quietly prayed for their school. Soon, others joined them and the revolution began.

Close to one hundred students joined in, including two other introverted students named Leah and Nathan. Grayson, Angie, Leah and Nathan, along with a few others, soon started what would later become the Patrick Henry Christian Student Club on campus, and the prayers of those students began to transform the school. That year our unranked boys' basketball team made it all the way to the state championship game. Two years later, attendance was up and suspensions were down. *USA Today* ran a story on some of the top high schools in the country, and Patrick Henry was mentioned. Some people will claim that the turnaround was due to a new principal, new teachers and a new attendance policy, but I say it was because two quiet students started praying weekly for their school.

I remember two other introverted students, Danielle and Justin, in the youth group at Park Avenue. Danielle was also part of that Christian student club at Patrick Henry. She was quiet but always showed up for just about everything that went on in youth group. Every chance I could I tried to encourage Danielle and Justin, though they hardly said a word in youth group. It would have been easy to ignore them both; I had to go out of my way to connect with them. With Danielle I would mention her name in front of the whole youth group and point out her quiet leadership at Patrick Henry. With Justin I would spend time playing video games as a way to connect. When I was invited to be a trainer at DCLA, a Youth for Christ conference, I was asked to bring two student leaders with me to help in the training. I brought Danielle and Justin, my two quiet leaders. They both seemed surprised that I would invite them to go with me to Washington, D.C., and allow them to share about their faith in their own way.

Today Danielle attends the church that I pastor and is a part of our worship and creative arts ministry, sharing through her passion and gifts in spoken word and poetry. She is also a student at the University of Minnesota and, with her soft-spoken voice, is quietly sharing her poetry and Jesus with others.

Justin is working with an organization called the Youth Enterprise Foundation. This faith-based organization works with inner-city youth developing leadership and business skills. One of their businesses is a T-shirt printing business just two blocks from our church office in North Minneapolis.

When I think of and observe the ministries of Danielle and Justin, I think about the importance of not overlooking quiet young people and their potential to advance God's kingdom. This is a message that we must get out to our young people. They must know that they can make a difference, that they can build God's kingdom on earth right here and right now. They must know that they are not too young to be used by God to make a revolutionary impact in the world, that they can take on giant issues and see victory in the battle. We must let them know that they are special and gifted and that they can start a revolution! Even if they are quiet or shy, they can lead a silent revolution through their prayers. For God says that "where two or three come together in my name, there am I with them" (Matthew 18:20). It just takes a few to start a spiritual, kingdom-building revolution.

# 9

# COLLABORATION
## THE EMPOWERMENT OF YOUNG HEROES

When I left Ohio in the fall of 1999, I left a youth staff of three full-time people (including myself) and one part-time person and arrived at Park Avenue United Methodist Church in Minneapolis to find a youth staff of one—me. It was lonely those first few months, not because the rest of the church staff wasn't encouraging to me, but because I was so used to having other people around to talk, pray and strategize with about youth ministry. There were issues that came up in just my first few months at Park Avenue that I didn't have the capacity to address on my own.

It was because of those issues that I first sat down with Wiley Scott from Twin Cities Young Life, Noelle Palmer of Community Ministry in South Minneapolis and Chris Brooks, who at the time was a volunteer youth minister and working full time at a local high school. I met with them because I wanted to have some other youth workers to pray with. Little did I know what our weekly prayer meetings would become.

After one of our meetings, during which we prayed for our ministries, our city and our personal needs, Noelle told us that she felt that God was calling us to do more than pray together.

Wiley, Chris and I felt the same way; we just weren't sure at the time what we were to be doing. We also felt that we needed to invite other urban youth leaders to our times of prayer and fellowship. So, we began to strategize and imagine what could be.

One day Wiley shared a Scripture with us that laid the foundation for what would eventually come of all our prayer, dreaming and strategizing: "I have given them the glory that you gave me, that they may be one as we are one: I in them and you in me. May they be brought to complete unity to let the world know that you sent me and have loved them even as you have loved me" (John 17:22-23).

Those words challenged us in a powerful way. We realized that we needed a place where youth workers who didn't have the resources, budget or staff to pull off a holistic urban ministry on their own could support and minister to one another, thus equipping them to more successfully work within their ministries. With that Scripture as our basis, we embarked on a collaborative approach to youth ministry, believing that we could accomplish more together than we could accomplish alone.

Initially we were thinking of this collaborative ministry only in the context of the urban environment. In the city many churches do not have the resources that their suburban brothers and sisters have, yet the young people they are called to reach seem to bring more issues, barriers and challenges to the table than do suburban youth. A collaborative approach was a must if youth ministry in the city was going to be effective. But, as I meditated on our foundational verse, I came to realize the importance of unity regardless of geographic location. Ministries need collaboration for the sake of the unity God calls the body of believers to model. What message do we send to un-churched people when they see how divided the church is? What image do they have of God when they see the disunity of his children? A collaborative approach to youth ministry that includes churches of all geographic locations and ethnicities first and foremost allows the world to see what a difference Christ really makes. By the unity and love that youth ministers show for one another, it sends a message about our connected-ness to God (see John 13:35). Then, through that unity, we are able to accomplish great things together.

The idea of collaborative youth ministry was not new to me. I had actually encountered it years before I began to meet with Noelle, Wiley and Chris.

## HOSPITALITY HOUSE

From 1993 to 1996 I worked for Hospitality House Youth Direc-tions, a parachurch ministry in North Minneapolis, and it was there that I met Elwood Jones. Originally from the Washing-ton, D.C., area, he was a natural when it came to urban youth ministry. Through Hospitality House he conducted weekly gatherings called Teen Talk, as well as retreats and neighbor-hood outreaches.

But Elwood had a heart for something bigger than what one youth minister or one parachurch could do alone, so he invited youth ministers from the Minneapolis and Saint Paul areas to meet with him and discuss a vision he had for a city-wide youth gathering where there would be food, worship, music and a message relevant to urban youth and in which young people would play lead roles. The youth ministers at that meeting were sold on the vision, and Friday Night Live was created.

Once a month at a church in Minneapolis or Saint Paul there was a gathering of young people from all over the urban Twin Cities, and pretty soon even suburban youth groups began to come. Each service was followed by an after-party with activities such as roller skating, Christian dance parties or all-night lock-ins at a community center. Youth from all over the Twin Cities who normally wouldn't hang out with each other came together during those services and after-parties. It truly looked like a sneak preview of heaven (see Revelation 7:9).

Friday Night Live was a testimony of the love and unity among the youth ministers who had seen Elwood's vision and come together to make it happen. It demonstrated not only what the body of Christ *could* be but what it *should* be, and I believe that it empowered young people to be future builders of the authentic church. Many of the young people who attended asked us, "Why can't church be like this all the time?"

Out of Friday Night Live came a youth leadership retreat, which equipped young people to be leaders in their schools, churches and communities. It featured large group sessions as well as seminars and workshops geared toward empowering youth to be young heroes for God. In some cases the retreat enabled churches to equip the youth in their ministries in a way they couldn't on their own.

After that retreat Elwood began to share another big vision that he had for something called Hoodfest, an outdoor Christian hip-hop festival in the heart of the city. He met with the leaders in the Friday Night Live network and shared his idea of a stage set up right in the city that featured hip-hop groups, youth choirs and national youth speakers. He saw youth groups coming from the city, the suburbs and even the rural areas. He talked about bringing something of excellence, something that was full of the Spirit of God, to the inner city. He imagined holding workshops to further teach young people and a conference that would happen before the event so that youth could be involved as leaders as well. This conference would give youth the chance to invite others from their churches, cast a vision about the impact the event would have and train them in how to serve. Given the diversity of the youth who would attend, he wanted to focus on issues of reconciliation. As he talked, it was hard not to get excited and want to pull the whole thing off that very day. Later, when I looked out from the stage of Hoodfest and saw thousands of young people joined together, I understood the power of collaboration.

## CHANGED LIVES

When I think of the young people who were impacted through the collaborative approach at Hospitality House, I think of Chris Snoddy. Chris was involved in all the ministries and programs at Hospitality House, and after he graduated from high school he went on to earn a college degree from Tuskegee University in Alabama. Today, he is working in South Minneapolis as the director of a faith-based computer-learning center connected to the Urban Ventures Leadership Foundation. Could it be that through the collaborative approach of Hospitality House, along with the support of loving parents, Chris Snoddy was empowered to not only live the life of a young hero but to later serve in the community as an adult hero who is leaving a legacy as he touches the lives of urban youth?

It would have been difficult for Hospitality House, with one ministry or one person, to dream such big dreams and actually see them become realities. But, through a collaborative approach to youth ministry, we *can* dream big.

### MINISTRY MODEL

Loren Woods, who was educational coordinator of Hospitality House, collaborated with all seven Minneapolis public high schools as well as Young Life and Student Venture to develop a program called Career Exploration. The program was based within the schools and provided opportunities for young people to think critically about their futures through academic support (he created a database to track the young people's attendance and academic progress), field trips to the offices of doctors, lawyers, politicians and record label executives, and presentations from public school alumni who were now living out successful careers. Young people with potential who were falling through the cracks academically were recruited to participate in the program. It was Loren's dream that the young people who participated in the program would be inspired to dream about what they could become and then set goals to accomplish that dream, and many young people really were empowered through the program. This type of holistic and empowering model of ministry could not have been accomplished without a collaborative approach.

## URBAN RECLAIM

A few years later when I began to strategize with Noelle, Wiley and Chris it was hard for me not to remember Friday Night Live and Hoodfest. We knew that there was a need once again for a collaborative approach to youth ministry in the urban Twin Cities.

The first thing we did was to name to this new movement. We called it Urban Reclaim. From there, we began to contact other urban youth pastors who we thought might be interested in fellowship, networking, prayer and, eventually, collaboration. We began to hold weekly meetings in which we sat in a circle and talked about what was going on in our lives and our ministries and how others could pray for us. Today these meetings are monthly luncheons and training times that reach over forty urban youth ministers and other Christian youth workers across the Twin Cities. We have even been able to connect with some suburban youth workers as well, and we are not only reaching leaders from local churches and parachurches but from community centers and educational institutions as well.

A couple of years ago we began to envision a collaborative project that would empower urban youth to become young heroes for God. This led to the creation of a youth leadership retreat held during the Martin Luther King Jr. holiday weekend that features hip-hop praise and worship, national youth speakers and workshops for both youth and youth workers. The youth workers involved with Urban Reclaim serve as workshop leaders, lead skits and games and plan the themes of each year's retreat. For the first year each ministry was asked to bring five to ten young people from their ministry to the retreat, and only two years later over two hundred urban youth and thirty youth workers were being reached. By bringing youth ministries together across denominational, ethnic and church lines, we are giving young people a larger vision of what the church can be.

## ONE IN THE SPIRIT

By spending time with other youth ministers in prayer and discussion, I found myself becoming empowered as a youth minister. I learned that our ability to empower young people stems directly from the empowerment we receive through collaboration with our peers. In addition, I learned that when we are in collaboration, we can accomplish more in developing revolutionary youth ministry models than when we are alone. Collaboration challenges leaders to think more critically about their ministries and causes them to dream bigger dreams.

Our unity as the body of Christ is pleasing to God, and it paints a picture for young people of what the church can look like in the future. We must equip and empower them to build up a church that is relevant to the culture they live in without watering down the gospel. By getting young people involved in collaborative ministry opportunities that cross denominational, ethnic and church lines, we can empower them to reach their communities—and the world!

Collaboration is also a great way to see youth with leadership potential in your youth group as design partners and not just as ones whom you are always pouring into. What if God wants to use young people to pour into you? I know of a youth pastor who allows a small group of youth to pray for him weekly, to help him in preparing his talks and to plan events. When I was the youth pastor at Ginghamsburg Church, I had a group similar to this. We worked together to plan our monthly outreach called Madhouse Live. It was so cool to watch the youth themselves come up with creative ideas to reach their peers. They thought of things and raised issues that I probably never would have thought of on my own. Through this process the youth also felt a greater sense of ownership in the youth ministry. Shouldn't the youth ministry in some way ultimately belong to the youth themselves?

I believe collaboration between other ministries is important not just because it's a way to develop stronger and broader ministries when you're in a smaller church with limited resources but also because it exposes you to the larger body of Christ that transcends geography, race and denomination. Churches connecting in this way in my home city led to youth collaborating on their own to put on alternative parties on Friday nights, evangelism events in their high schools and Christian hip-hop concerts. It's powerful to see the larger body of Christ working together to advance the kingdom across a whole city!

# CONCLUSION

The culture we live in has changed. Youth ministry, however, hasn't changed all that much over the years.

*But wait,* you say. *Look at how professionalized youth ministry has become. Look at the large churches that now have multiple staff dedicated to ministering to youth. Look at all of the conferences that train and equip thousands of youth ministers every year. Look at the number of books written on innovative new aspects of youth ministry.* Well, this may all be true, but let me ask you this: Are all of these things relevant to today's youth in a way that truly ministers to them?

Youth culture today is rich in media that bombards young people with consumerism and graphic images of violence and sex. The divorce rate, absentee parents and the culture of individualism leave them feeling lonely, neglected and outcast. Paired with the influences of a corporate music industry that lifts up gangsta rap and the thug lifestyle, these elements are producing more and more at-risk youth—in the suburbs as well as the cities.

Today's youth are living in an urban, hip-hop-influenced culture, and many mainstream ministry organizations seem to be missing this fact. So many of these organizations are dominated by a suburban, white model of youth ministry, and as a result we aren't seeing many resources that speak directly to what is influencing today's youth culture and how we ought to address those issues. Suburban youth ministries stay on one side of the fence, and the urban ministries stay on the other. Unfortunately, this segregated youth ministry world is not prepared to deal with the emerging urbanized, hip-hop and multiethnic youth culture.

To be effective in reaching this generation of young people, youth ministries must become more holistic in their approaches. They must take into serious consideration the elements that are influencing young people and use them as vehicles to present the gospel. This means that ministries will have to change the way they relate to young people and the way they present life in God's kingdom on earth. These new models will take paradigm shifts, resources and a rethinking of theology, but the revolution that it will spark will make it all worth it.

We must continue to truly observe the culture that youth live in and be aware of the main influences within the culture. From here we must raise up young heroes who are in the culture but not of it. We do this through a holistic approach that reaches them spirit, soul and body. Intimacy with God is so important if young people are to live in the culture with their peers and not be of it. For them to get to this point they need to know that God loves them. Before anything else we must provide the opportunity for young people to get alone away from the busyness of life and experience the love of God. From here they need this reality of God's love to take up residence in every area of their life. Knowing that God has a plan for their life and that this loving God wants to use them in a revolutionary way right now can bring comfort to a young person's soul, but it can also be scary at the same time. This is why the consistent presence of an adult mentor is so important. Every young person should have a caring adult walking with them, serving as an earthly example of God's love—an adult who will help a young person work out what it means to live for Jesus in every area of their life, showing them what it truly means to see their body not as their own but as a temple of God.

In this challenging world that youth live in we must work to help youth see that they can make a difference right now and that they can find victory in the midst of struggle. We have a great opportunity to raise up young heroes for God, to have a ministry that is proactive about a developmental and holistic approach to youth ministry with long-term disciples as the goal.

Efrem Smith can be contacted to arrange speaking engagements through Kingdom Building Ministries. More information about Efrem and an audio sample are available at the Kingdom Building Ministries website: <<www.kbm.org>>. He is listed on their "Itinerant Speakers" page. Through his use of humor, storytelling and dissection of Scripture, Efrem clearly communicates messages focused on racial reconciliation, lifestyle choices and the heart of missions.